Regulating
International Business
through
Codes of Conduct

Regulating International Business through Codes of Conduct

Raymond J. Waldmann

American Enterprise Institute for Public Policy Research
Washington and London

Raymond J. Waldmann is an attorney in private practice in Washington, D.C. He was formerly staff assistant to the President and deputy assistant secretary of state for economic and business affairs, heading the U.S. delegation to over thirty negotiations, including those on the Liner and Technology codes.

Library of Congress Cataloging in Publication Data

Waldmann, Raymond J
    Regulating international business through codes of
conduct.

    (AEI studies ; 287)
    Bibliography: p.
    1. Trade regulation.   2. International business
enterprises—Law and legislation.   3. International
economic relations.   4. United States—Foreign economic
relations.   I. Title.   II. Series: American Enterprise Institute for Public Policy Research.   AEI
studies ; 287.
K3941.W34   341.7′5   80-19846
ISBN 0-8447-3392-X
ISBN 0-8447-3424-1 (pbk.)

AEI Studies 287

Printed in the United States of America

What we are paying for four hundred years of white im-perialism—and how long, to all appearances, we shall go on paying! Asians and Africans do not forget and are so far from forgiving that, if they can thereby do some harm to the ex-imperialists, they will blithely damage them-selves, even commit suicide. If I can spite your *face, I will cut off* my *nose. There is no appeal from these passions even to self-interest. Indeed, if people would only act ac-cording to their self-interest, this world would be almost a paradise.*

ALDOUS HUXLEY
Letter to Juliette and Julian Huxley
January 27, 1957

Contents

Introduction

As this work deals with an aspect of U.S. foreign policy, it should be axiomatic that U.S. interests will be given primary consideration. In examining codes of conduct, we must be concerned with their impact on the U.S. economy, on the U.S. position abroad, on U.S. investors and multinational corporations, and on U.S. consumers.

Our country's own interests should not be the only consideration, however. Even if a code of conduct would have an adverse impact on U.S. interests, there may be valid reasons for supporting it. One should look closely at benefits to other countries and interests, especially if these benefits tend to increase world political stability. Direct benefits flowing from codes of conduct have been claimed; they include an increase in world trade, greater competition in world markets, faster development of poor countries, and increases in standards of living. These claims must be weighed by U.S. policy makers and negotiators along with the more immediate and tangible benefits flowing from U.S. investment abroad: a healthy and strong U.S. economy and continued access to needed raw materials and resources—benefits to the United States which could be affected by codes of conduct.

We must be concerned with the achievement of the broader objectives of U.S. foreign policy, difficult as it is to define them. These objectives evolve through our continuous interaction with other countries and through the domestic political process. In the international economic field, we must be concerned with the economic well-being of our allies, the security of our important resource suppliers, and the development of better relations with our adversaries. These groups also constitute real or potential competitors in international trade and investment; the greatest competition comes from our closest allies.

We should, however, guard against attempting to achieve these broader foreign policy objectives at any cost. The reduction of tensions may not always be sufficient justification to reach an economic agreement against our interests. Other governments are often very explicit in seeking economic advantage. Congressional expressions of concern about the Panama Canal, our relations with China and Taiwan, the power of the third world in the United Nations, and other similar issues all have fundamental economic content. Congress sees these as reminders that the United States should, on some occasions, be prepared to step away from an international agreement rather than to accept a bad one.

This work emphasizes the issue of the legal implementation and enforceability of codes of conduct, reflecting another of the author's concerns. Governments should not, as a general rule, pass laws or negotiate agreements that cannot be enforced. It is poor public policy to raise expectations about goals that cannot realistically be attained. Enforcement and implementation are particularly important issues in international organizations, where a code could theoretically be adopted by a majority made up of developing countries over the objections of the countries most affected by its provisions. The disputes that could result from such a lack of consensus would not only be a diplomatic failure, but could also fuel further resentments on the part of developing countries.

Nevertheless, there is a continuing U.S. interest in creating useful and effective international institutions and regulatory regimes. If these institutions and regimes follow U.S. models and proposals, so much the better. We can argue convincingly that laws and policies that have been good for the United States may also help other countries, and codes of conduct may be one way of sharing this experience. One should not, however, argue for wholesale adoption by others of U.S. law in fields such as antitrust, nor justify negotiating positions on such an outcome. We should recognize that codes of conduct can raise regulatory consciousness in other countries and that this result may benefit U.S. businessmen in their competition with those from previously less regulated economies. Thus codes of conduct may perhaps confer unintended benefits on the United States in the long run.

The discussion will focus upon the development of codes of conduct and upon the issues and policy choices facing the international community. It reflects the status of code negotiations through 1978, before the conclusion of negotiations on several of the codes under consideration, including the Code on Restrictive Business Practices. Chapter 1 seeks to identify some of the concerns associated with the operations of multinational enterprises and to demonstrate the importance to U.S. policy makers of current efforts to regulate international business transactions. Chapter 2 examines the under-

2

lying trends in the international economy that have shaped the development of codes of conduct. The following chapter attempts to identify some of the relevant legal characteristics of codes. Chapter 4 examines recent precedents in the creation of codes of conduct and the next three chapters describe the major directions of several efforts now under way. The final chapter suggests some guidelines for U.S. policy in dealing with codes of conduct.

1

Business Regulation: A Major Problem of International Economics

During the 1970s, a major new international economic problem emerged: the regulation of international business activity. This problem is a major concern of government officials. It has been highlighted by popular writers. The issues have been analyzed by academic and legal scholars from many countries and points of view. It has occupied much of the time of diplomats in international organizations. Actions now being debated will affect our way of life and standard of living for the rest of this century and beyond.

The problems associated with multinational enterprises originate in three broadly shared concerns. First, countries object to interference in their domestic political affairs by multinationals with allegiances elsewhere, if anywhere. Second, countries object to the "rape" of their natural resources, symbolized by the export of raw materials to be made into finished products for import at what they see as excessively high prices. Third, developing countries claim imbalances in bargaining power when dealing with multinational enterprises on economic matters.

Even the legitimacy of multinational enterprises (MNEs, or more usually, multinational corporations, MNCs) has been called into question.[1] As one commentator succinctly asked:

(1) By what right do MNE's gain their alleged economic power? To whom does the generated wealth really belong?

---

[1] Terminology in this field is not settled. The United Nations consistently uses the term "transnational corporation" and the abbreviation TNC. The OECD, on the other hand, uses the term "multinational enterprises" and the abbreviation MNE. The more standard term in common usage is "multinational corporation," or MNC. No particular significance should be given in this work to the use of any of these terms. It is perhaps important to use the term "enterprise" rather than "corporation" to emphasize the need to include state corporations and state business entities in any definition when this is appropriate.

(2) By what right do MNE decisionmakers in headquarters located in one country allocate resources that affect the wealth and welfare of citizens in other countries? (3) To whom are MNE's accountable? What publics? What body politic? At home and abroad?[2]

It is generally agreed that there is little likelihood that MNCs will be subject to the authority of a comprehensive international regulatory organization in the near future. It is no wonder, therefore, that great attention is now being paid to establishing codes of conduct to regulate particular actions of multinational enterprises. Codes of conduct have been seen as an alternative means to constitute an international moral authority by international agreement among governments, to help nation states solve their problems, and to provide guidelines for multinational business activities.[3]

The Importance to U.S. Policy

A U.S. policy maker might be tempted to ask the relevance to the United States of efforts to regulate international business transactions. Is not our country still the strongest economy in the world and in a position to control or even ignore undesirable developments? Are we not able to isolate ourselves from the adverse effects of decisions in other countries or blocs? Don't we have the strength, resources, and technology to command respect and attention for our policies?

If such a proposition were ever true (and it may have been most nearly true immediately following World War II), it is no longer. Although we are still a leader in the world economy, in defense, and in international organizations, we no longer enjoy the same dominance in international matters we had two or three decades ago.

We still have substantial interests, however. We are a major factor in international business. In 1975 multinational corporations produced over 25 percent of the world's goods and services, with U.S. multinational firms responsible for about 60 percent of this total.[4] But American multinational corporations are not without vigor-

---

[2] Howard V. Perlmutter, "Perplexing Routes to M.N.E. Legitimacy: Codes of Conduct for Technology Transfer," *Stanford Journal of International Studies*, vol. 11 (1976), p. 170.

[3] Paul M. Goldberg and Charles P. Kindleberger, "Towards a GATT for Investment: A Proposal for Supervision of the International Corporation," *Law and Policy in International Business*, vol. 2 (1970), p. 295. The United Nations, Department of Economic and Social Affairs, "The Multinational Corporations in World Development" (ST/ECA/190), 1973.

[4] Foreword by L. L. Morgan to *The Case for the Multinational Corporation*, ed. Carl Madden (New York: The National Chamber Foundation, 1977), p. ix.

ous and aggressive competitors from all parts of the world. In international negotiations with Europe and in the industrial nations' Organization for Economic Cooperation and Development (OECD), as well as in dealings with our hemispheric partners, with our emerging allies and trading partners in Asia and Africa, or even with the Soviet bloc, we face increasingly strong competitors, new challenges, and decreasing influence. As a result of these changes, U.S. policy making must take into account not only the increasingly competitive international environment, but also the increasing economic interdependence of the countries of the world.

In simple terms, we can no longer isolate our economy from those of others. We import and export too much. Our currency is no longer

TABLE 1

DIRECT FOREIGN INVESTMENT IN U.S. AND U.S. INVESTMENT ABROAD

(book value in billions of dollars)

Investor	1960	1965	1970	1975	1977
Canada					
U.S. investment abroad	11.2	15.3	21.0	31.2	35.4
Foreign investment in U.S.	1.9	2.4	3.1	5.1	6.0
Western Europe					
U.S. investment abroad	6.7	14.0	25.3	49.6	60.6
Foreign investment in U.S.	4.6	6.1	9.6	16.5	22.7
Other Countries					
U.S. investment abroad	14.0	20.2	29.9	48.4	58.2
Japan	0.3	0.7	1.5	3.3	4.1
Other developed countries	1.2	2.3	4.1	7.0	8.0
Latin America	8.4	10.9	13.0	22.2	27.7
Middle East	1.1	1.5	1.5	−4.5	−3.1
Other less developed countries	1.6	2.8	4.7	8.1	9.1
Unallocated	1.4	2.0	4.5	7.2	7.0
Foreign investment in U.S.	0.3	0.3	0.6	5.1	5.4
Total					
U.S. investment abroad	31.9	49.5	76.2	129.2	148.8
Foreign investment in U.S.	6.9	8.8	13.3	26.7	34.1

NOTES: Minus sign indicates liabilities exceed assets. Columns may not add to totals because of rounding.

SOURCE: *International Economic Report of the President*, transmitted to the Congress, January 1977; *Survey of Current Business*, August 1978; *Statistical Abstract of the United States*, 1978.

regarded as the world's monetary standard; it is only one of the basket of currencies making up the assets of the International Monetary Fund (IMF) and its member countries. Our economy increasingly relies on imported crude oil and raw materials, payment for which depends more and more on our exports of food, manufactures, and services.

Our trade deficits are to some degree being offset by flows representing income to U.S. corporations, such as the dividends paid by foreign corporations to their U.S. corporate parents; the royalties and fees paid by foreign licensees, including U.S. subsidiaries to U.S. patent holders and trademark holders; and the earnings derived from banking, insurance, transportation, and other service industries. Fur-

TABLE 2

U.S. Receipts and Payments for Transfer of Technology—Royalties and Fees

(millions of dollars)

	1965	1970	1975
Receipts			
From Canada			
Investment related	185	311	540
Noninvestment related	26	33	37
From Western Europe			
Investment related	381	675	1,587
Noninvestment related	189	247	343
From Japan			
Investment related	20	66	200
Noninvestment related	66	202	227
From Australia, New Zealand, South Africa			
Investment related	59	90	177
Noninvestment related	17	23	37
From All Other Countries			
Investment related	279	419	730
Noninvestment related	37	68	115
Total	1,259	2,134	3,993
Payments to All Other Countries			
Investment related	68	111	241
Noninvestment related	67	114	192
Total	135	225	433
Net Surplus	1,124	1,909	3,560

Source: Chamber of Commerce of the United States, *Technology Transfer and the Developing Countries* (Washington, D.C., April 1977).

ther, direct investment is becoming a two-way street, with increases in U.S. investment abroad being partly offset by foreign investment in the United States (see table 1). U.S. investment abroad is generally at much greater risk than foreign investment here, and we therefore have an interest in retaining an international system in which these transactions occur securely and predictably.

A particular income flow, payments for technology, has become more important to the United States, one of the world's few net exporters of technology. In 1975 we received about $4 billion for royalties and fees, paying out only $433 million (table 2). Although much of this income is investment related, we show a significant surplus on the much smaller noninvestment-related accounts as well (table 3).

TABLE 3

NONINVESTMENT-RELATED U.S. RECEIPTS AND PAYMENTS FOR TRANSFER OF TECHNOLOGY

(millions of dollars)

	1965	1970	1975
Western Europe			
Receipts	189	247	343
Payments	61	99	168
Balance	128	148	175
Japan			
Receipts	66	202	227
Payments	1	4	8
Balance	65	198	219
Developing Nations			
Receipts	37	68	115
Payments	2	7	8
Balance	35	61	107
Other Countries			
Receipts	43	56	74
Payments	3	4	8
Balance	40	52	66
Total			
Receipts	335	573	759
Payments	67	114	192
Balance	268	495	567

SOURCE: Chamber of Commerce, *Technology Transfer and the Developing Countries.*

In spite of the erosion of the U.S. position in the international economy, the United States still exercises substantial moral and political leadership. Most of the developed Western countries continue to assert, even if they no longer fully believe, that the U.S. position is decisive in multilateral diplomacy. Many developing countries regard the United States as a model. Our own laws and policies are often viewed as the "wave of the future" for other countries.

The United States must firmly exercise the leadership with which it has been entrusted. U.S. policy makers must take heed of current efforts to regulate international business activities and must carefully analyze the new codes of conduct that those efforts have spawned. These novel regulatory devices mark an important new direction in international relations. They arise from an acute dissatisfaction with past relationships and a bold disposition to reorder the course of future relations. They cannot be treated lightly. The United States must act to ensure that any new international agreements do not conflict with our own best interests or with those of a peaceful and prosperous world.

To assess the development of codes of conduct, we must understand the underlying trends of international economic affairs and the environment in which decisions about codes of conduct will have to be made. These trends and the issues surrounding them are examined in the next chapter.

2
Current Trends in International Economic Affairs

Codes of conduct have not developed in a vacuum, but rather reflect events and interests of national and international scope. Some of these events and interests have arisen or been shaped in direct response to the activities of the multinational corporation. Others are unrelated to the subjects of the codes per se, but are products of transcendent political and ideological forces. Their impact on the codes has been perhaps the most intense.

Four trends have had the greatest effect on the development of codes of conduct. They are:

- the increasingly important role of governments in economic affairs
- the increasing politicization of governmental economic policies
- the increasing concern for the impact of international economic policies on development in the less developed countries (LDCs)
- the increasing awareness of and concern for secondary effects of international economic policies and activities

Role of Governments

Governments are increasingly participating in the direction and regulation of international economic affairs. Some of these actions are stimulated by domestic pressures and by domestic regulatory policies, but in other cases international regulation has a life of its own. Although the United States is now questioning the necessity for extensive regulation of some industries, it has long had a pervasive government regulatory structure. A few of the advanced countries of Europe have followed the United States in regulating domestic business activity, but generally to a lesser extent. Governments elsewhere have not regulated either domestic or international activity to the same degree

11

as has the United States, but they now seem to be moving in that direction. Moreover, regardless of their domestic regulatory practices, governments everywhere are increasingly concerned about private international commercial and economic affairs.

Recently, the interest in regulation has manifested itself in intense efforts to extend the international regulatory sphere to commercial and investment activities not previously controlled. These efforts frequently assume two familiar and well-established forms: bilateral treaties and multilateral conventions. Bilateral diplomacy is the approach with the greatest appeal for the United States. When dealing with most other countries on a bilateral basis, we were able to exercise greater influence because of our greater economic strength. Basic to our bilateral economic ties are treaties of friendship, commerce, and navigation, which the United States has entered into with sixty-eight countries. Although their terms vary, these treaties generally provide that U.S. citizens and corporations will receive either the same treatment in the signatory country as nationals of that country or no less favorable treatment than nationals of other countries. These treaties have been supplemented by specialized bilateral agreements covering such subjects as customs treatment, withholding of taxes, import and export marketing arrangements, transportation agreements, and many similar technical arrangements.[1]

The web of bilateral agreements is complex; no two countries enjoy the same pattern of arrangements. Variations must inevitably occur even in subjects of apparent technical uniformity. In matters where uniformity is sought, multilateral diplomacy has long been used to achieve agreement among nations. What is now being urged by advocates of codes of conduct, however, departs from the trends of the past in two respects.

First, while many of the bilateral and multilateral treaties that are in force today affect private corporations, in fact they express that impact in terms of governmental rights. For example, a U.S. bilateral aviation agreement, by its own terms, specifies rights of each nation (not airlines) to land civil aircraft at points within the other nation. Similarly, bilateral tax treaties define how the states treat taxes and taxable income, irrespective of the effect of such taxes on particular

---

[1] The United States had, according to the U.S. State Department, 3,311 bilateral treaties in force in 1975. The greatest number were with Canada (186), the United Kingdom (128), the Philippines (89), Japan (85), West Germany (79), France (69), Italy (68), Greece (64), and Mexico (64). The United States was party to bilateral treaties with 135 of the 154 countries recognized by the United States as of that date. E. Plischke, *Microstates in World Affairs* (Washington, D.C.: American Enterprise Institute, 1977), p. 62.

firms. Conventions frequently are simply agreements to enact reciprocal national laws governing, for example, recognition of foreign
patent filings or grants. While these agreements certainly affect the
business opportunities of private persons, they do so by regulating
intergovernmental transactions or by prescribing governmental treatment of private parties. There is now, however, a distinct trend toward
the development of treaties that concern themselves with hitherto
private international transactions and decisions, thus bringing contracting governments into fields not previously regulated by international agreement.

Second, one may further distinguish between agreements that
establish international organizations with an independent existence
and those that do not. A large number of technical, multilateral agreements dealing with customs cooperation, patent validity, trademark
recognition, vessel loading standards, pollution, fishing rights, and so
forth, do not necessarily lead to the establishment of permanent
organizations. In some cases, new international organizations are
created, but these organizations have traditionally served as clearing-
houses for information, monitoring the activities of signatory nations.

In recent years, and especially since the United Nations adopted
the New International Economic Order (discussed below), the LDCs
in particular have pressed for the creation of international organizations to enforce new multinational agreements. Proposals of the UN
Centre on Transnational Corporations, the Law of the Sea Conference,
and the United Nations Conference on Trade and Development
(UNCTAD) give international organizations the mandate of directly
intervening in international business affairs. International bodies may
be empowered with the authority to rap the knuckles of companies
acting outside international agreements. International organizations
may also be authorized to interpret agreements through some system
of administration and review. They may further provide for settlement
of disputes through conciliation, arbitration, or even adjudication.
Codes of conduct would continue and even reinforce this kind of
institutional intervention.

Politicization of Economic Policies

The politicization of international economic affairs is perhaps inevitable given the increasing role that governments play in them. Once
governments deal with economic matters, many concerns including
political ones begin to enter into negotiations. Foreign ministers sometimes treat economic issues as mere bargaining chips in a larger game.
Economic policies become parts of overall "packages" of policies,

developed and often negotiated by diplomats with little experience in or understanding of the business realities involved. There is consequently always a danger that the underlying commercial and economic interests will be submerged or even ignored.

One of the results of growing government involvement in economics has been the emergence of an economic diplomatic corps, dealing largely with itself, at conferences in Geneva, New York, and elsewhere. As a result of their previous foreign service, these diplomats may be familiar with the realities of diplomacy and foreign relations, but few have more than a simplistic view of the operation of the private sector. This is more true of the representatives of the less developed countries than of the developed ones. There is, accordingly, a need for diplomats to maintain contact with representatives of private interests who understand the commercial transactions affected by government policies. The need is seldom met.

Although many in this economic diplomatic corps may lack an understanding of international business, they do not suffer from a lack of new ways to politicize international economic affairs. To further their development goals, the LDCs have begun to use their voting strength in "one country, one vote" international organizations and the economic strength of oil-exporting members of the third world. The most outstanding example in recent years was the passage by the UN General Assembly in 1974 of resolutions to establish the "New International Economic Order" (NIEO) and the related Charter of Economic Rights and Duties. Both were approved over U.S. objections. The resolutions expressed the intention of developing countries to assert sovereignty over their national economies and natural resources. They declared a "right to reparations" from the developed world and stated in rather explicit terms the actions expected of the international community to assist the developing countries.

If these were actions that could be taken without cost to other countries, there would be no legitimate objection to them. The problem with the NIEO is, however, that it tends to view the world's riches as a fixed pie which must be cut up in another way. The issue is purely political: who gets what. If the international community were to adopt policies based on this theory, not only would development in the rich nations be hampered, but the economies of many of the developing countries would stagnate even further. The increasing politicization of economic issues has already been detrimental to the expansion of world trade and investment. The more serious difficulty is that there is no evident limit to the degree to which economic affairs may be further politicized.

Unfortunately, current efforts to create codes of conduct are products of this politicization process. They are largely political responses to economic problems. The proposals, past and pending, on technology transfer are based on the notion that the relative bargaining positions of the haves and have-nots need to be changed through law, without providing incentives to actually increase the amount of technology being transferred. In addition, the efforts to regulate multinational enterprises are often merely a convenient distraction from the domestic causes of social and economic injustice. Further, legislation of LDC market shares in the exports of goods and services such as shipping, aviation, banking, and insurance is advocated as a matter of right, without regard to available opportunities to borrow both the expertise and the capital that could earn market strength in those industries. The continued politicization of economic problems could have adverse consequences for those countries advocating it most vigorously.

Concern for Development

The less developed countries, now numbering 109 of the 149 members of the United Nations, have long linked their international economic diplomacy to their overriding concern for domestic economic development. They tend to view every measure through this prism, and they systematically reject proposals that do not at least promise to contribute to development.

In recent years, the LDCs have asserted their concerns in efforts to stabilize or enhance mineral and other commodity export prices and to regulate the transfer of technology. The Organization of Petroleum Exporting Countries (OPEC) is the most visible and successful of these efforts. Its members have rapidly progressed from being less developed countries to becoming some of the wealthiest nations in the world.

Perhaps to emulate the OPEC countries, other less developed agricultural and raw material exporters have banded together to determine other commodity prices. Commodity agreements have been negotiated in sugar, chocolate, and coffee, among other exports. More recently, LDCs have urged the creation of a common fund to support the price-setting agreements of a number of separate commodities, and serious negotiations have been under way with the developed nations to establish such a fund. This effort has been opposed, though, by many who believe it will introduce new rigidities and costs into international trade not present in a more competitive environment.

Many nations have also seen controls on the transfer of technology as a means to achieve rapid development. Mexico, Brazil, Portugal, and the members of the Andean Common Market are among the nations that have pursued this route. Through regulation of the transfer of technology, they have attempted to increase the relative benefits accruing to their countries in transfer agreements and to screen out unwanted investment. But while these regulations may increase benefits to the host country if and when technology is imported, they may prove counterproductive by inhibiting transfer.

Partly because of the successes of these limited efforts, or perhaps equally because of their failures, representatives of the LDCs have begun to advocate negotiation of international codes of conduct as a means to generalize these development efforts on a worldwide scale. Some of the codes, such as the UNCTAD guidelines on restrictive business practices, or the UNCTAD Code of Conduct on the Transfer of Technology (discussed in chapter 6), deal with subjects already intensely regulated in several countries. Others expand the limits of the law into new fields. All are perceived by the LDCs to be essential to development. Codes of conduct have become the new focus of the developing nations in their search for a panacea to their economic woes.

Although concern for development is understandable, not all questions can or should be answered by reference to their development impact alone. Furthermore, there is little agreement on what in fact leads to successful development. A preoccupation with the short-term impact of policies on the balance of payments, the creation of jobs, or the growth of gross national product could be destructive in the long run. For example, a country may succeed in temporarily improving its economic position by nationalizing an industry, then find that it attracts no new investment in that or any other industry. As a result, its technological base could wither away for lack of interchange with the more advanced world. Development policies having the effect of introducing barriers to investment or trade will tend to be self-defeating.

The basic problem is that the goal of development may in fact be illusory. It is certainly not politic to suggest that some countries may never develop, given their culture, background, or resources. There may be international variations on a theme of economic Darwinism: Some countries were "born poor" and may be destined to remain relatively poor for the foreseeable future. Moreover, many developing countries have failed to use their resources wisely or to put their own houses in order—to reduce the stranglehold of the semi-feudal land-owning and money-lending classes and to reduce gross postcolonial economic disparities and corruption. It is considered interference in domestic affairs for outsiders to point to these matters, but failures continue to mount. Development has quickened in LDCs, but not as rapidly as the increases in the developed nations; the gap is still widening. Poverty, malnutrition, and other ills still prevail. Therefore the urge to provide remedies through government action, such as through codes of conduct, will also continue.

Concern for Secondary Effects

The fourth trend in international economics is an increasing awareness of the side effects of development and a desire to avoid the adverse ones. In the past, economic development policies ignored their effects on urban areas, on the distribution of wealth, and on the environment. Now, the LDCs are basing arguments on their perception of environmental impacts, and they are being aided by some developed countries like Canada with similar problems and concerns.

There are both dangers and opportunities in this increasing awareness of the side effects of development. The danger is that excessive concern for secondary effects can itself have adverse economic and social effects. It can stop growth, increase regulation, and deter new initiatives. The opportunities are for us to point out our own valuable experiences.

We have not yet used our opportunities to describe and document in the international community the adverse impact of regulation on our own development. For example, at the UN conferences on the environment (Stockholm 1975), population (Romania 1976), and habitation (Vancouver 1976), we adopted a party line that more, not less, governmental regulation is the answer to these problems. Perhaps we can reverse this trend to indicate instead the problems associated with government intervention and excessive regulation. But given bureaucratic inertia, such a reversal is unlikely without substantial effort.

It is equally important not to ignore the side effects of LDC demands. Any transfer payments—"reparations," price supports, soft loans, or whatever—can increase worldwide demand. Government-dictated increases in prices of oil, sugar, or bauxite may be offset by improvements in the technologies and efficiencies of production and distribution, but only to a degree. After that, increased costs will "push" prices while increased demand "pulls" them. The inevitable result will be lower disposable income in developing countries.

. . .

These trends portend great changes in our current international economic system. We are on the threshold of creating a broad, bureaucratic, and possibly unmanageable international regulatory structure. This structure is being justified in the United States because it could accelerate economic development in the poorer nations, harmonize disparate national laws, and bring foreign business regulatory standards into line with our own.

On the other hand, any such structure contains the seeds of increased uncertainties, delays, and costs. There is always the potential for abuse of administrative power. Uncoordinated and contradictory decision making and the restriction of private activity in the name of "public purpose" are probable results. Public purposes are rarely well defined; in fact they are discretionary, highly political, and often no more than catch phrases for darker motivations. One must be concerned about the creation of any conditions under which such tendencies flourish. Codes of conduct must be examined guardedly to ensure that they advance rather than obstruct the economic system upon which we all depend.

3
The Legal Nature
of Codes of Conduct

Although the term "code of conduct" has been used in international organizations for many years, there is no single, precise, or widely accepted definition of its meaning. Most users of the term appear to know generally what they intend, but the term has not yet been defined in either national or international law. The United Nations Commission on Transnational Corporations formulated a program of work on a code of conduct without defining it. Other organizations have also adopted the term, usually without formal definition. The first use of the term "code of conduct" has not been identified in UN reports, in reports of other discussions, or in the literature on international codes of conduct.

The term "code" is rather ambiguous and has no single established legal usage. A code may be a source of new law or it may be a compilation of existing laws. In a national legal context, the term "code" usually refers to a more-or-less systematic compilation of laws and decrees. On the international level, it has been used to characterize a systematic arrangement of rules in a given field.[1] Thus the term has been applied to an arrangement of conventions and recommendations (by the International Labor Organization in its "International Labor Code" of 1957); to agreements defining the rights of combatants in war and in captivity; to rules established by negotiation in an international organization (by the OECD); and to a negotiated convention (the UNCTAD Code of Conduct on Liner Conferences; see chapter 5).

One discussion of the meaning of "code of conduct" is found in

---

[1] United Nations Economic and Social Council, *International Codes and Regional Agreements Relating to Transnational Corporations: A Comparative Survey of Selected International Instruments*, Report of the Secretariat, Commission on Transnational Corporations (E/C.10/9), January 30, 1976.

the report of the UN's Group of Eminent Persons set up in 1972 to discuss the problems of multinationals. In the Group's report, a code of conduct is defined as ". . . a consistent set of recommendations which are gradually evolved and which may be revised as experience or circumstances require. Although they are not compulsory in character, they act as an instrument of moral persuasion, strengthened by the authority of international organizations and the support of public opinion."[2] Most developing countries have adopted the position that codes of conduct must and should be binding and capable of enforcement. If those to whom the code is addressed abide by its terms voluntarily, then no enforcement mechanism would be required. Enforcement by international institutions, by national laws, or by other mechanisms, however, would be entirely consistent with the nature of a code, though not as the Group of Eminent Persons has defined it.

Codes of conduct cannot be easily categorized in the traditional terms of international law because codes have both private and public aspects. They clearly deal with the rights and duties of private persons, but they also address standards for so-called legal behavior of states. Thus both public and private actions may be regulated in a single code. One commentator has concluded that codes of conduct demonstrate the error of past definitions separating international law into public and private domains.[3] A code provision directing private corporations abroad not to act as instruments of their home governments involves a governmental as well as a private purpose; unless the home government also abides by the prohibition, the private corporation could be subject to conflicting governmental policies.

The problem of the nature of a code of conduct is not solved by looking to the nature of the promulgating organization. Codes are being adopted by international organizations (such as the United Nations and its specialized agencies), by regional intergovernmental organizations (the OECD and the Andean Group), and by private groups (such as the International Chamber of Commerce). Even individual companies are promulgating "codes of conduct" to guide employee behavior.

Internationally negotiated codes of conduct could be incorporated into national law. It is clear that once a code of conduct is incorporated into national law by specific legislative act or by accession

---

[2] United Nations, Department of Economic and Social Affairs, *The Impact of Multinational Corporations on Development and on International Relations* (E/5500/Rev. 1 ST/ESA/6), 1974, p. 55.

[3] Seymour J. Rubin, "Harmonization of Rules: A Perspective on the United Nations Commission on Transnational Corporations," *Law and Policy in International Business*, vol. 8 (1976), p. 876.

to or ratification of an international document, it will have binding effect before national courts. If the code itself provided an international enforcement mechanism, it could have effect in international law and perhaps even in national courts.

There is ample precedent for the notion that both an agreeing state and its public and private entities will be bound by the restrictions and provisions of a convention or other international instrument to which that nation has adhered. The major international conventions dealing with transportation, communications, postal service, patents, and similar matters set standards by which both public and private institutions operate; these standards are accepted by large numbers of states who often disagree on political issues. Some of the more important agreements and institutions created by them are listed in table 4.

Even in the absence of a formal act of adherence to an international convention, there is considerable pressure for a state to observe, and to force its citizens to observe, internationally established rules. These pressures may be as effective as formal adherence in attaining conforming conduct. This is evident in the almost universal observance of well-entrenched customary international law, such as rules on criminal jurisdiction on vessels in territorial waters.

Codes go further, however, in binding citizens of nonadhering countries. For example, if states A and B agree to a code of conduct to govern the operations of transnational corporations in their territories, these provisions would be binding on all operations in state A or B, including those of citizens of state C, whether C agreed or not. If the agreement between states A and B contravened customary international law, the issue as to which law controls could arise in an international tribunal or in the national courts of A, B, or C, perhaps with different results. Similarly the code might conflict with treaties between C and A or B—such as treaties of friendship, commerce, and navigation. Further, if a code of conduct sanctions discrimination against foreign corporations whose activities do not meet code standards, an adhering state's action under the code may violate other multinational agreements, such as the General Agreement on Tariffs and Trade (GATT). Resolution of such conflicts would be difficult and the results unpredictable.

Purposes of Codes of Conduct

Codes of conduct can be negotiated to achieve various purposes, such as:

- establishing agreement between governments on rules of governmental conduct

TABLE 4

INTERNATIONAL INSTRUMENTS RELATING TO SPECIFIC AREAS OF ACTIVITY

Area	Instrument
Trade	General Agreement on Tariffs and Trade
	United Nations Conference on Trade and Development (UNCTAD)
International finance	Articles of Agreement of the International Monetary Fund and International Finance Corporation
Capital movements	Code of Liberalization of Capital Movements issued by the Organization for Economic Cooperation and Development (OECD) Council
Labor	Conventions entered into under the auspices of the International Labor Organization
	Recommendations of the International Labor Conferences
Technology transfer	The Paris Convention for the Protection of Industrial Property
	The European Patent Convention
	UNCTAD
	The Andean Group
Restrictive business practices	UNCTAD
	Decision 24 of the Andean Pact
	The European Economic Community Treaty
	The OECD
Transport	Various conventions adopted through multilateral conferences
	United Nations and UNCTAD activities
Environment	UN Conference on Human Environment
	Intergovernmental Maritime Consultative Organization
Consumer activities and protection	Various international instruments adopted by conferences
Settlement of disputes	Statute of the International Court of Justice
	Convention on the Settlement of Investment Disputes between States and Nationals of Other States
	Various rules for commercial arbitration
	United Nations
	Economic Commission for Europe
Company laws and regulations	The Common Market
	The Andean Pact

SOURCE: UN Economic and Social Council, "International Codes and Regional Agreements Relating to Transnational Corporations," UN Document E/C. 10/9/ Add. 1, February 3, 1976, pp. 16–34.

- harmonizing national laws and regulations
- supplementing national laws
- providing internationally accepted models for national laws
- increasing the effectiveness of national laws
- providing alternative ways to subject private enterprise to public and governmental policies

Perhaps the most important potential benefit of a code is the harmonization of national laws and regulations. Because businesses today face widely divergent regulatory regimes in different countries, varying greatly with economic or legal systems, and reflecting disparate cultures and states of development, compliance is costly. But, as worthy as the objective of harmonization is, it is unlikely to be achieved. Even after agreeing to an international convention, different countries will apply it differently; enabling legislation, administration, and enforcement will vary widely from country to country. Perhaps the most striking example of this is the Andean Investment Code (see chapter 4). If a group of five Latin American countries with relatively common culture, background, and heritage cannot achieve harmonization, one can imagine the difficulty of harmonizing laws of countries with more varied heritages and at different stages of development.

Codes may also have the effect of supplementing national rules of conduct, especially where it is impossible for a country to establish rules for itself. A government may be unable to legislate through its national assembly or parliament, but may achieve the same end by international agreement. It may be unwilling to take the risk of making its investment climate less attractive than that of its neighbors. It may even be unwilling or unable to take steps to intervene in its economy or to gain control over its resources without some outside help or stimulus.

A code may not only supplement existing national rules but might provide a model for future national legislation. Codes may enhance the effectiveness of national legislation by providing mechanisms outside the national jurisdiction for dealing with problems with which the state is concerned. In regulating complex international tax, trade, and other transactions, one state cannot deal with all aspects of the problem itself, and an international standard promulgated through a code may provide the answer. For example, the OECD Code for Multinational Enterprises or the proposed UN Transnational Corporation Code may allow signatory countries to regulate a transaction at both ends in concert. Such a step may have been beyond the powers or even the desires of the host country in which one invests in the absence of a commitment by the home country of the investor to assist. Financial and tax transactions would also be more easily regulated with the introduction of identical or similar reporting requirements at both ends of the transactions.

Finally, codes could provide new ways for countries to subject private enterprises to public policies. Corporations doing business in LDCs may find, for example, that the terms and conditions under which they do business will be substantially changed in favor of an LDC's economy or its own enterprises. The corporation may find that it has to take on a local partner, that its patents and trademarks are to be shared or its royalties restricted, or that its properties are subject to expropriation or nationalization for certain violations of law. To carry on its operations, the corporation may have to seek approvals from several government agencies, creating a potential for abuse. An important measure of progress from the viewpoint of the developing countries is precisely the degree to which the terms and conditions of trade and transactions are changed. There is no necessary limit to the kinds of policies that a country may assert to that end.

It is apparent from these examples that codes may be negotiated to achieve many objectives. Some codes, such as those which harmonize existing laws, may be concluded to facilitate international transactions. Others may seek to control transactions through increased national and international regulation. In a discussion of the scope and substantive provisions of various international instruments, the UN Secretariat's report to the Commission on Transnational Corporations concluded that it is difficult to draw useful distinctions between attempts to facilitate and attempts to regulate.[4] Characterizing provisions along these lines, the report asserted, tends to polarize thought without adequately reflecting the complexities of reality. In the domestic context, it is not uncommon for public agencies created to regulate a particular industry to turn into promotional agencies. It could be argued that this is in fact one purpose of such regulations— to save an industry from itself. Nevertheless, it is useful to keep in mind whether the overall purpose of an instrument is to facilitate the activities or subjects of its concern, or whether its purpose is to limit or control them.

Implementation and Enforcement

Most existing international instruments concerned with the conduct of transnational corporations limit themselves to statements of certain

---

[4] UN Economic and Social Council, *International Codes and Regional Agreements*, p. 5.

general standards. A few instruments play supportive roles by laying down procedures and rules for settling disputes. Still a third group of instruments prescribes concrete rules regarding activities in specific areas, and thus comes closest to prescribing laws and regulations that can be enforced. Obviously, these different kinds of instruments require institutional and procedural structures of widely varying complexity to implement and enforce their provisions and to amend or clarify their texts. Such structures may include:[5]

- institutional organs for formulating more detailed rules
- institutional arrangements for modifying the substantive provisions of the instruments
- machinery for imposing sanctions
- machinery for settling disputes
- machinery for obtaining and disseminating information
- enforcement organisms with supranational competence
- compliance monitoring without direct enforcement powers

At their simplest, international instruments may contain no machinery for implementation. In many cases no execution or implementation machinery is necessary or desired. Some multilateral conventions provide for a minimum of machinery, including procedures for amendment or revision. Such machinery is often supplied by means external to the instrument, through an international organization, periodic consultation and review, or other means. In some cases dispute settlement mechanisms are expressly incorporated by reference to other organizations, such as the International Court of Justice or the International Chamber of Commerce, for arbitration.

International instruments that have legally binding form usually provide for some machinery to settle disputes. Articles 164 through 188 of the Treaty of Rome establishing the European Economic Community (EEC), for example, set forth the structure and jurisdiction of the Court of Justice of the European Communities. The member states agree that the court has jurisdiction over issues relating to the actions of the EEC council and commission, over the failure of member states to fulfill their obligations under the treaty, and over the content of certain council regulations. The court also has jurisdiction to interpret the treaty when such matters are raised in cases before national courts of member states. A number of multilateral conventions provide for similar jurisdiction by the International Court of Justice, but many states have entered reservations with respect to those treaty provisions. Disputes can also be settled through administrative or quasi-

---

[5] Ibid., p. 19.

judicial organs created within the particular international instrument itself.

Binding arbitration is another dispute settlement mechanism used in some international instruments. States, individuals, and enterprises use arbitration as a means to resolve differences amicably. Arbitration is often preferred over traditional judicial proceedings because it is relatively fast, often is less formal, and usually employs arbitrators whose expertise in the subject of the dispute is greater than that of judges on national and international tribunals. For this last reason, arbitration is especially desirable in highly technical matters. The largely unused Convention on the Settlement of Investment Disputes between States and Nationals of Other States establishes an arbitration procedure.

A final option for dispute settlement is conciliation. The parties agree to meet with conciliators in the hope of achieving a mutually acceptable settlement. Conciliation rules have been provided by the International Chamber of Commerce. An interesting application of conciliation in a code is found in the UNCTAD Convention on a Code of Conduct for Liner Conferences (see chapter 5). By providing for "international mandatory conciliation," even though parties are not bound by the finding of the conciliator unless they so agree, the parties are encouraged to reach agreement.

In most treaties, noncompliance by a state that is a party to the instrument may be considered a breach of the state's obligations. Under international law, the state would then be subject to sanctions such as the payment of damages, the suspension or termination of the treaty, or the freeing of other parties from their obligations.[6] Some multilateral instruments provide that a state that does not comply with its obligations must notify the other parties to the convention. This provision is used in the General Agreements on Tariffs and Trade, the convention of the OECD, and the International Monetary Fund Articles of Agreement. Some bilateral treaties provide for notification and require negotiations or consultations upon request of the other party. The provisions of treaties addressed to individuals or legal persons are usually enforced through national legal systems of the states that adhere to such instruments; the sanctions for noncompliance are indicated either in the international instrument or in national law. Nonbinding international instruments usually contain no enforcement machinery. In these cases, "sanctions" could only

---

[6] Stephen Coonrod, "The United Nations Code of Conduct for Transnational Corporations," *Harvard International Law Journal*, vol. 18, no. 2 (Spring 1977), p. 300, note 140.

include persuasion and public opinion. Of course, nonbinding instruments can be and are cited as standards of behavior in arbitration or negotiation and could affect the outcome of a dispute.

Conclusion

It is clear by their terms that codes of conduct purport to regulate activities of private persons. They specify rules of behavior to which penalties for violation may attach, and which have distinct consequences under national or international law. Codes of conduct with enforceable standards for private behavior are potentially powerful devices.

The following chapter examines two recent precedents in the development of codes of conduct. The first is a regional code, binding upon its signatory states and capable of national enforcement. The second is a voluntary set of guidelines drafted by the developed nations, establishing standards of corporate behavior. An examination of the successes and failures of these existing codes will permit more penetrating analysis of those codes of conduct still being negotiated.

4

Recent Precedents

The negotiation of major new international regulatory instruments has only recently become a reality. In the last decade, the negotiation of several instruments similar to codes of conduct has dramatized the significance of the movement to regulate international business activity and has established important precedents for codes of conduct still under consideration. Two particular efforts deserve fuller treatment. These are the Andean Investment Code and the OECD code for multinational enterprises.

The Andean Investment Code

The group of decisions and agreements comprising the basis for the Andean Common Market provides a common regime for investment and divestment, propounds standards against which business practices will be judged for restrictiveness, and alters the terms and conditions under which investment in the Andean countries may take place and technology may be transferred. Its importance lies in its uniqueness. It was the first regional agreement to include provisions similar to those now advocated for a transnational corporation code of conduct.

Background. The Latin American Free Trade Association (LAFTA) and the Alliance for Progress led to the formation of the Andean Common Market (ANCOM). LAFTA was established in February 1960 by the Treaty of Montevideo[1] to increase the regional exchange of goods among its signatory nations and to make more effective use of

---

[1] The LAFTA nations were Argentina, Bolivia, Brazil, Chile, Colombia, Ecuador, Mexico, Paraguay, Peru, Uruguay, and Venezuela.

the continent's natural resources. The wide gap between the most-developed and the least-developed LAFTA countries contributed to the lack of progress toward achieving an integrated program. The "big three" in LAFTA—Argentina, Brazil, and Mexico—substantially increased their exports to other LAFTA countries and attracted most new foreign investment, while Chile, Colombia, Ecuador, and Peru experienced continuing and substantial trade deficits. The Alliance for Progress, created by the Punta del Este agreement in 1961, supplemented regional resources with public and private funds from the United States. Although one of the original objectives of the Alliance was "to strengthen existing agreements on economic integration," the approaches of LAFTA and the Alliance were never coordinated.[2] As a result, the most highly developed countries received the greater proportion of new foreign investment.

To attempt to solve the regional problems stemming from the trade barriers associated with LAFTA and to improve their developmental planning, the Andean countries created a subregional group within LAFTA. In the Bogotá Declaration of August 1966, Colombia, Chile, Peru, Ecuador, and Venezuela announced their intention to form an Andean Common Market to promote regional development through economic integration and private foreign investment. They emphasized the need for regional development planning including "complementation agreements" and joint venture projects between signatory countries.[3] With the addition of Bolivia in 1967, they attempted to form a reasonable economic counterweight to the "big three."[4]

Negotiations on a common code to regulate foreign investment were consummated in May 1969. The delay was a result of a split of the ANCOM members into two groups: the free trade group, consisting of Colombia and Chile (with support from Bolivia), and the "evolutionary group," made up of Peru, Venezuela, and Ecuador. The evolutionary group expressed a long-felt discontent in Latin America, particularly resentment toward American multinational corporations.

[2] Frances Armstrong, "Political Components and Practical Effects of the Andean Foreign Investment Code," Stanford Law Review, vol. 27 (July 1975), p. 1598.

[3] Complementation agreements provide for the manufacture of different complementing products in any particular industry by signatory parties, and, consequently, for the duty-free exchange of such goods from one country to the other. See ibid., p. 1599, note 11.

[4] During the years 1969 and 1970, the GNP of the Andean Group, including Venezuela, was $31.2 billion as against $21 billion for Argentina, $33.7 billion for Brazil, and $31.6 billion for Mexico. Annual Report, Inter-American Development Bank (1971), as quoted in Stanley R. Lisocki, "The Andean Investment Code," Notre Dame Lawyer, vol. 49 (December 1973), p. 319.

U.S. investment occupies a commanding position in Latin American economies. As of December 1969, 40 percent of all manufacturing exports from Latin America were produced by U.S. firms.[5] Foreign-owned industry produced almost 14 percent of the total gross domestic product of Latin America, an amount difficult to ignore. Further, the evolutionary group generally felt that U.S. investment preempts opportunities otherwise open to the local investor-manager.

The more highly industrialized Andean countries, which were more likely to benefit from trade liberalization, crossed swords with those countries in a less competitive position. The agreement which finally emerged in May 1969, informally known as the Cartagena Agreement, was a concession to both sides as it provided for both trade liberalization and industrial planning. The agreement committed the Andean group to develop a common investment policy, a major part of which was to be an investment code. Venezuela, influenced by strong private industrial, commercial, and agricultural interest groups, withdrew from the group rather than agree to the compromise.

The Andean Investment Code, promulgated as decision 24 of the Andean Common Market, included the first multinationally agreed program of divestment. The scheme, proposed years earlier by Professor Paul Rosenstein-Rodan, is based on a belief that equity investment by foreigners means higher costs for the host country than do other forms of investment, because the equity investor expects a higher return than does the lender. Therefore, it is advantageous for a developing country to reduce the foreigner's equity interest in his investment.[6] The concept of phasing out foreign equity investment was developed further by A. D. Hirschman in November 1969.[7] He proposed an International Divestment Corporation that would, with international financing, buy out foreign firms and sell them to local investors.

The Andean Code's controversial divestment provisions required foreign firms to form joint ventures or to offer at least 51 percent of

---

[5] The importance, in terms of concentration of U.S. investment, was more pronounced. In December 1969, of the $20 billion invested by the United States in less developed countries, more than $5 billion was invested in the Andean Common Market countries, or about 25 percent of all U.S. investments in the third world. This included a disproportionate amount of $2.67 billion in Venezuela.

[6] P. N. Rosenstein-Rodan, "Philosophy of International Investment in the Second Half of the Twentieth Century," in *Capital Movements and Economic Development*, ed. J. Adler (New York: St. Martin's Press, 1967), as quoted in Armstrong, "Andean Foreign Investment Code," p. 1603.

[7] A. D. Hirschman, "How to Divest in Latin America and Why," *Princeton Essays in International Finance*, no. 76 (1969), as quoted in Abelardo Lopez Valdez, "The Andean Foreign Investment Code: An Analysis," *Journal of International Law and Economics*, vol. 7, no. 1 (June 1972), p. 4.

their shares for purchase by national investors within ten to fifteen years of the time the code came into force. The proposal again split the Andean group in two and jeopardized the entire integration effort. Peru, Chile, and Bolivia supported divestment while Colombia and Ecuador wanted less controversial provisions. The Andean Code was finally approved at the December 1970 meeting of the Andean Common Market Commission[8] and came into force within a year.

The Andean Code was regarded by U.S. investors with suspicion. Soon after its promulgation, the Council of the Americas conducted a survey of companies doing business in Latin America to assess the expected effects of the proposed investment code on U.S. investors. Of the fifty-six companies responding, fifty-one indicated that the investment code would discourage their investment in the Andean Common Market.[9] This message was not lost on some Andean countries.

Political changes in each of the Andean countries also critically affected the solidarity crucial to the program. The constitutional crisis in Colombia in 1972, the overthrow of the Allende government in Chile in September 1973, and the alignment of the new Chilean government position with the previously installed conservative military governments in Bolivia and Ecuador all weakened the strict nationalistic control over foreign investments favored by the elements present during the creation of the Andean group. The new military government in Chile favored an extremely liberal economic policy, including low and uniform common external tariffs. This government gave preference to market mechanisms for the allocation of resources and mistrusted sectoral programs of industrial development. Most importantly, it opposed any special regulations for foreign investment.

After further negotiation within the Andean Common Market, a compromise was reached in the form of a protocol modifying the Treaty of Cartagena. Chile and Colombia agreed to an extension of the trade liberalization program until 1982 and the other members agreed to reforms in industrial programming. Although this seemed to satisfy all parties, Chile in August 1976 refused to sign the protocol agreement and was forced to withdraw. The code remained in effect for the other five states, however, and continues to exert morally persuasive power in the thinking of other developing countries throughout the world.

---

[8] The Andean Foreign Investment Code was approved on December 31, 1970. Officially, this agreement is decision 24 of the commission (ANCOM's governing body) and it is entitled "Common Rules Governing the Treatment of Foreign Capital, Trademarks, Patents, Licenses, and Royalties."

[9] Lisocki, "Andean Investment Code," p. 330.

Provisions. The Andean Code was drafted as a single document, reflecting not only theoretical interests and political pressures, but also various compromises. The code puts together, for the first time, a series of provisions dealing with multinational corporation activity. It defines three types of enterprises: (1) national enterprises, with more than 80 percent of the capital belonging to investors who are nationals of the Andean Pact countries; (2) mixed enterprises, in which 51 percent to 80 percent of the capital is owned by national investors; and (3) foreign enterprises in which less than 51 percent of the capital is in the hands of national investors. The code requires that these percentages be reflected in the technical, financial, administrative, and commercial management of the enterprise. This provision in effect bans contracts that give foreign minority investors control of companies owned by a majority of nationals.

All new foreign investment undertaken after July 1, 1971, requires prior approval of the government in which the firm is located. According to one observer, "Decision 24 has launched the world's first multistate or regional system of prior restraints on the entry of new private sector investment from outside their combined territories."[10] Investments will be allowed that are development related, are not adequately covered by existing enterprises, are not takeovers of shares or rights owned by national investors, and are not in a sector closed to foreign investors.

The Andean Code also places restrictions on certain sectors, prohibiting new foreign investment in public services, insurance, commercial banking, domestic transportation, radio, television, and newspapers, for example. It restricts foreign investment in "domestic marketing of products of any kind," a new and perhaps self-defeating position. Existing enterprises in these sectors must convert, according to the provisions of the Andean Code, to national enterprises within three years from the date the code enters into effect. In contrast, the extractive industries, particularly oil and gas exploration, and international transportation are not so restricted.

The incentive for transforming foreign enterprises is the provision, under article 27, of tariff-free trade within the Andean community only to those enterprises which are "national" or "mixed." Reduction of the foreign element to no more than 49 percent must occur by the end of fifteen years in Colombia, Peru, and Venezuela, and by the end of twenty years in Bolivia and Ecuador. The differen-

---

[10] Covey T. Oliver, "The Andean Foreign Investment Code: A New Phase in the Quest for Normative Order as to Direct Foreign Investment," *American Journal of International Law*, vol. 66 (1972), p. 777.

tial recognizes the less developed status of Bolivia and Ecuador and their need to rely on foreign capital for a longer period of time. The Andean Code does not rule out nationalization or other takings, but it does provide for sales of ownership interests to the state or state enterprises as well as to private individuals. In fact, given the scarcity of local private capital, many observers have noted that state enterprises and government institutions are most likely to be the buyers of divested shares. Sales are to be controlled by a competent national authority, an agency that presumably will review the value and method of determining the value of the shares at the time of the sales. The state may also be a purchaser. Verified profits resulting from investment not exceeding a 14 percent return annually may be repatriated.

Important and novel restrictions on remittances of royalties and fees for technology are imposed, and the code also broke new ground here. Foreign trademarks may be subject to special charges for their use in free market trade. Furthermore, article 25 provides that trademark agreements may not contain clauses requiring the licensee to use raw materials, intermediate goods, or equipment supplied by the owner of the trademark.

Article 20 prohibits a number of restrictive business practices and thus introduces "antitrust" considerations into the Andean legal framework. Restrictions on licensees to use property within a specific territory are prohibited. In addition, the national authorities are to look at the contribution to the national economy of goods incorporating imported technology, although the standards and procedures for doing so are not specified. Royalties are constrained in two cases: If they relate to "know-how" they must be reviewed by the control agency; if they are furnished to a parent or an affiliate by a foreign enterprise, they may not be a deductible expense. Article 20 also outlaws certain business practices that are commonly prohibited in the United States such as tying clauses, resale price maintenance, production restrictions, prohibitions on competitive technology, and charging royalties on unused patents in a package.

Foreign Response. The early analyses of the Andean Code tended to take its provisions at face value. Many commentators, such as the respondents to the early Council of the Americas survey, saw the code as a comprehensive and universal investment code that would adversely affect investment and would be applied uniformly throughout the region. For U.S. investors, however, experience has shown that the impact may have been more psychological than real. Government statistics have not yet indicated a significant decline in existing investment, nor has there been a decline in the rate of new investment.

Respondents to a Harvard Business School survey[11] in 1971 felt the formulation of the Andean Code was too theoretical. They found it was drafted in haste and with loose wording that would impair its effectiveness. Half of those interviewed felt the decision would not be ratified. They pointed to long-standing rivalries, cultural and political differences, and lingering desire for sovereignty over development and use of natural resources as factors that would militate against ratification. They saw decision 24 as a polemic—a strong declaration of control over foreign investments for nationalistic, largely political reasons. Several respondents thought that the Andean Code could not be implemented and that some features would stop the inflow of foreign capital, slow down economic development, and create untenable political pressures. The experience of Mexico was cited as precedent. None of the respondents saw any immediate opportunities being offered by the opportunity to trade in a new Andean Common Market, in contrast with the earlier experience with the European Common Market.

All of the respondents felt the transformation or divestment provisions to be impractical. American companies were not going into business to go out of business. They felt that these provisions would adversely affect existing American business and that future direct investment would be drastically reduced. Although many respondents were willing to consider entering into joint ventures, in practice such operations pose difficult and sometimes insurmountable problems. Native Andean businessmen expect high dividends and quick returns and thus are unwilling to invest in long-term projects. Joint ventures are also costly and major consumers of management time, particularly where basic differences in business philosophy and style prove obstacles.

The respondents further believed that the Andean Code would encourage the growth of government bureaucracy for purposes of asset valuation, investment registration, and technology description. At a minimum, they perceived that this would precipitate large amounts of paperwork; at worst, it could lead to administrative abuses, discretionary behavior, and opportunities for corruption. Instead of providing a more certain environment in which to plan, the Andean Code, in the view of many of the respondents, just created more uncertainties.

In interesting counterpoint to their general views, however, individual plans of action of the respondents were not expected to be

---

[11] "How Will Multinational Firms React to the Andean Pact's Decision 24?" *Inter-American Economic Affairs*, vol. 25 (Autumn 1971), p. 55. The respondents included representatives of four banks, three petrochemical companies, three mining concerns, one insurance company, and nine manufacturing companies.

greatly affected. The U.S. banks interviewed were not concerned with direct restrictions; most were willing to accept local investment in varying degrees. While three banks had no plans for expansion, one had such plans and was adhering to them. Seven of the nine manufacturing companies interviewed expressed willingness to accept a minority interest in the Andean Pact area if forced to do so by governments. Only one company thought that joint ventures provided obstacles to transfer of technology, but all were concerned with control of operations under joint ventures. One company was pulling out of the area because of lack of market rather than because of the Andean Code. For the mining and oil companies, there was little impact.

The survey authors concluded that although American business was unhappy with the code, no major shift of present investments was likely to occur. Executives were likely to react to the regulation rather than act on the "opportunities" of the common market. If there were an opportunity to make a reasonable return on an investment, the code would not deter future investments.

Impact. As experience with the Andean Code has grown, commentators have seen differences appear within ANCOM; political changes in Chile and Venezuela, in particular, have contributed to weakening unity among the member countries. Some countries have introduced new antitrust and business practice concepts, especially in the area of limitations on royalties payments to foreign licensors. One commentator concludes that our interest in the Andean Code and the ancillary national regulations stems from the fact that they mark the first enactment by the Latin American countries of a body of antitrust laws that is intended to be applied immediately and with full force and effect.[12]

There is little doubt that the Andean Code was intended to change the balance of bargaining power between licensor and licensee. Traditionally, Latin American economists have emphasized the imbalance between "those on different ends of the technology transfer bargain." According to Latin Americans and economists throughout the developing world, the bargain has traditionally been adverse to the developing country. Early concession and licensing agreements were by their nature likely to lead to bad deals. One way to solve this problem for the developing country is never really to seal the bargain. Codes and national laws alike often require that past license

---

[12] Lawrence F. Ebb, "Transfers of Foreign Technology in Latin America: The Birth of Antitrust Law," *Fordham Law Review*, vol. 43 (April 1975), p. 722.

agreements as well as new ones be subject to review and revision. The government becomes a third party at the bargaining table. It will be increasingly difficult in these circumstances to agree to binding terms with licensees on the basis of trademarks without expiration, patents with long lives, or means of controlling know-how. The Andean Code institutionalizes the tactics of continuing bargaining.[13]

Not surprisingly, the individual countries are applying the code in different ways. There is no uniformity of national enactment, national regulation, administration, or even definitions. Furthermore, differences in other domestic laws passed both before and after the code was ratified create substantially different situations in different countries. Stanley Rose concludes that "without more uniformity of opinion in regard to what the code means and the existence of a higher tribunal to which any party in interest could have recourse, the code will continue to be the disincentive to investment that it presently is. The rules of the game have been fixed and are generally acceptable. It is their varying application which bothers the players."[14]

With the exception of the special case of Peru, where other government policies had discouraged investments before the adoption of the code, direct foreign investment into the Andean countries has not stopped. Indeed, one observer asserts that the flow of foreign direct investment to the region has increased.[15] This is not to say that the code has achieved its objective of reducing dependency, but on the other hand, it has not had the dramatic adverse impact forecast for it. Companies will invest in the area if they have a reasonable expectation of profit and some certainty of repatriating investment and profits. Furthermore, the divestment requirement acts as a safety valve against all-out expropriation and could contribute to a stable investment climate. To one observer the code seems to be a good bargaining tool for the member countries and a starting place for regulating foreign investment.[16]

The Andean Code may yet prove, in the long run, to be the stabilizing factor that has long been needed to provide the foreign investor with a favorable investment climate. It can contribute to the development of the Andean region. It can also contribute to the economic integration of Latin America if the Andean countries begin to operate as an economic unit. Rather than discouraging economic

---

[13] Harlan M. Blake, as quoted in appendix to ibid., p. 729.

[14] Stanley F. Rose, "The Andean Pact and Its Foreign Investment Code—Need for Clarity?" *Tax Management-International Journal*, vol. 1 (January 1975), p. 16.

[15] Sven Heldt, "The Decay of the Andean Group," *Intereconomics*, no. 3/4 (1977), pp. 72–78.

[16] Valdez, "The Andean Foreign Investment Code," p. 16.

development through foreign investment, the Andean Code could provide the conditions necessary for such development.

The OECD Code for Multinational Enterprises

The second recent effort deserving detailed examination is the OECD's code for multinational enterprises. The Organization for Economic Cooperation and Development is a twenty-four nation intergovernmental organization composed of the developed countries of the free world. Reflecting concern for the void left by past futile efforts and wishing to forestall more drastic measures, the OECD Council of Ministers formed a Committee on International Investment and Multinational Enterprises in January 1975.[17] Within eighteen months, the committee drafted a series of documents: a declaration on international investment and multinational enterprises, including guidelines for multinational enterprises, and intergovernmental agreements on equal treatment for foreign investors and on official investment incentives and disincentives. The documents are addressed to both member countries of the OECD and to multinational firms operating within them.

Declaration. Adopted on June 21, 1976, the OECD declaration acknowledges the important role multinational enterprises play in international investment and emphasizes the contributions they can make to the economic and social progress of OECD member nations. It states that member countries should treat enterprises from another member the same way they treat domestic firms. The declaration recognizes, however, that member countries have a right to regulate both the entry of foreign investment and the conditions of establishment of foreign enterprises. This qualification was included at the request of Canada and Australia. With respect to investment incentives, the member countries agree to endeavor to make such measures as transparent as possible so that their importance and purposes can be ascertained. Finally, members agree to consult on these matters

---

[17] The Organization for Economic Cooperation and Development is a Paris-based group of twenty-four nations formed in 1960 when the United States and Canada joined with eighteen European nations. Member countries now include Australia, Austria, Belgium, Canada, Denmark, Finland, France, Germany, Greece, Iceland, Ireland, Italy, Japan, Luxembourg, the Netherlands, New Zealand, Norway, Portugal, Spain, Sweden, Switzerland, Turkey, the United Kingdom, and the United States. Yugoslavia has special status. The OECD is dedicated to three basic principles: long-term economic growth of its member countries, expansion of world trade, and assistance to the less developed nations. The participating countries comprise only 20 percent of the world's population, yet represent 60 percent of its industrial production, 70 percent of its trade, and 90 percent of its aid to developing nations.

and to review them within three years. The full texts are presented in appendix A.

Guidelines. The OECD Guidelines for Multinational Enterprises constitute a voluntary code of conduct for such firms and contain a series of general normative policies.[18] The guidelines are not legally enforceable and do not displace local laws and regulations. They are explicitly limited to multinational enterprises operating within the territories of OECD member countries, but the document extends a "welcome" to other states to cooperate in this field. The guidelines are to be interpreted in the light of different problems in different countries. To avoid potential discrimination against multinationals, they suggest that both multinational and domestic companies be subject to the same expectations.[19]

The first guidelines on general policies basically direct enterprises to be good citizens. Multinational firms should cooperate with governments, give consideration to government policies, cooperate with local community and business interests, hire locally where possible, and not bribe or attempt to corrupt public servants.

The guideline on disclosure of information has proven to be one of the most controversial, perhaps because it actually requires someone to do something. It directs enterprises to publish information about their structure, activities, and policies, and to issue financial statements and pertinent information dealing with the ownership of the company, the areas of its operations, sales and operating results by geographical area and by line of business, new capital investment, statements of sources in uses of funds, employment, spending on research and development, policies for intragroup pricing, and accounting policies.

The implications of these disclosure requirements have been spelled out for U.S. companies by the U.S.A. Business and Industry Advisory Committee to the OECD (BIAC). BIAC finds that in view of financial reporting now required within the United States by the Securities and Exchange Commission, the New York Stock Exchange, and by accounting principles, the disclosure guidelines in the OECD

---

[18] All are preceded by the phrase, "enterprises should."

[19] Although the introduction states that a precise legal definition of a multinational enterprise is not required, it goes on to state that MNEs usually comprise "companies or other entities whose ownership is private, state, or mixed, established in different countries and so linked that one or more of them may be able to exercise a significant influence over the activities of others and, in particular, to share knowledge and resources with the others." Annex to the Declaration of 21st June, 1976, paragraph 8.

code should not burden U.S. companies. U.S. companies, though, could face new requirements for reporting employees, operating results, new capital investment on a geographical basis, and intragroup pricing policies. BIAC concludes, ". . . the U.S. multinational should find that its present annual reports for shareholders and for SEC filings provide a satisfactory basis for voluntary recognition of the OECD recommendations for information disclosure."[20]

The guidelines with respect to competition are so general and unexceptional that it is hard to see precisely how a company would alter its behavior, presuming it already adheres to U.S. law. These guidelines require, for example, that companies and enterprises "refrain from action which would adversely affect competition in the relevant market by abusing a dominant position of market power." The guidelines suggest that anticompetitive acquisition, predatory behavior, or anticompetitive abuse of industrial property rights could constitute such actions, without defining any of the terms and without setting standards for characterizing such behavior. This contrasts markedly with the efforts to define restrictive business practices in the UNCTAD Technology Code, where more specificity and potential enforceability have already been achieved.

The section on financing is very short, asking enterprises to take into account the objectives of the countries in which they operate regarding balance of payments and credit policies. In the taxation section, the guidelines suggest that enterprises obey the law when supplying information and engaging in transfer pricing. Companies should conform to the "arms-length standard" in transfer pricing.

The guidelines dealing with employment and industrial relations boil down to compliance with local law, tempered by the observance of standards "not less favorable than those observed by comparable employees in the host country." Companies should supply information about operations to employees and should recognize the right of employees to organize and bargain, where consistent with national laws. Since it is clear the guidelines do not override national laws, they provide no new rights or obligations either for enterprises or employees.

The final section dealing with science and technology suggests that enterprises should contribute to national scientific plans and capacities, allow for rapid diffusion of technology, and grant licenses on reasonable terms and conditions. It is hard to imagine that any

---

[20] "A Review of the OECD Guidelines for Multinational Enterprises: Disclosure of Information," USA-BIAC Committee on International Investment and Multinational Enterprise, November 1976, p. 21.

enterprise would feel constrained to alter its behavior on the basis of such provisions.

The promulgation of the guidelines was accompanied by a supportive letter from the secretaries of state, treasury, and commerce, and by educational activities of the U.S. Chamber of Commerce, BIAC, and other groups. As a State Department spokesman stated at the time, "The U.S. objective, a liberal climate for international direct investment, is unchanged. But the approach required to sustain this objective in the current environment is no longer total laissez-faire, but rather the creation of multilateral structures for cooperation and restraint on unilateral action."[21]

Consultation. Three decisions of the OECD council spell out consultation procedures for member states. The first says the OECD Committee on International Investment and Multinational Enterprises will review the guidelines and experience gained in their application. The committee can also serve as a forum for solving problems arising from conflicting requirements of member countries, but the activities of particular enterprises will be outside the scope of these reviews. The second decision, on national treatment, could have greater effect since it provides that if a member takes an action inconsistent with national treatment, it must notify OECD within sixty days; consultations may then be requested by a member country with respect to that action. The third decision requires similar consultations at the request of a member country that considers that its interests may be adversely affected by the investment incentives or restrictive measures taken by another country. These decisions will be reviewed within three years for the purposes of possible revision.

Impact. With only a few years' experience with the OECD code, it is difficult to determine what effect, if any, the guidelines have had. To show their good intentions, multinational firms are increasing the amount of information published along the lines specified in the guidelines and are demonstrating concern about meeting the disclosure "requirements." The guidelines have received wide dissemination and discussion within the United States, and some companies are making sincere efforts to act in accordance with them. But the preservation of a liberal economy as well as progress in the dialogue between the

---

[21] Paul H. Boeker, deputy assistant secretary of state for economic and business affairs, *Wall Street Journal*, May 28, 1976, as quoted in "A Review of the Declaration on International Investment and Multinational Enterprises," USA-BIAC Committee on International Investment and Multinational Enterprise, November 1976, pp. 22–23.

have and have-not states depend upon more—they depend upon avoiding the excesses of multinational enterprise behavior. Even though the OECD code does not apply to operations in developing countries, the guidelines may yet prove a useful standard for the activities of multinational enterprises worldwide.

The OECD code's provisions are not nearly as restrictive as those being considered within UNCTAD and the United Nations. Furthermore, the restrictions already in place in certain countries go well beyond the restrictions and standards set among the OECD countries themselves. The code does, however, provide guidance for the assessment of the legal effect of codes of conduct and background for the negotiations now under way at the United Nations.

. . .

The following three chapters examine several codes now before the international community. The first is the recently negotiated UNCTAD Code of Conduct for Liner Conferences. Although adopted by an UNCTAD conference in April 1974, it has not yet been ratified by a sufficient number of states to bring it into effect. Nevertheless, it is important not only as the first-adopted universal, worldwide code but also as the first binding convention drafted under the aegis of UNCTAD.

Two other codes now being negotiated are of potentially greater importance and of broader applicability. These are the Code of Conduct for Transfer of Technology, also being negotiated in UNCTAD, and the Code of Conduct for Transnational Corporations, under discussion at the United Nations. Both will have significant impact upon national legislation in developing countries whether or not they are ever successfully negotiated or adopted. They may make new law, though perhaps through a less satisfactory process than one would wish; they will, in any event, influence future relations of governments and multinational corporations. All three codes provide examples of the way in which the international community is dealing with the problem of regulating business and economic activity through codes of conduct.

5

Code of Conduct for Liner Conferences

One of the major concerns of developing countries has been the role international shipping has played in their economies. Many developing countries have traditionally depended upon foreign-owned vessels to carry their exports and imports. Paying for these services in foreign currency has contributed to balance-of-payments problems. In an attempt to improve this situation, a Committee on Shipping was formed in UNCTAD in 1965 to examine the basic assumptions of the ocean transport system in an atmosphere the developing countries hoped would be conducive to change.[1]

Between 1965 and 1975, the absolute tonnage of developing countries increased by 60 percent, but their share of total world shipping tonnage declined.[2] Currently, about 7 percent of the total world liner fleet sails under developing country flags. The announced objective of these countries was to achieve a 10 percent share by the end of the 1970 decade.

To improve their position in the liner segment of shipping, the developing countries have had to contend with the long-established position of shipping conferences. Conferences began in the United Kingdom. They are essentially cartels of shipowners who agree on rates and conditions of service. The first was an informal organization of shipping lines in the U.K.-India trade, dating from 1875. The example was followed in other trades.[3] The U.K. Royal Commission

---

[1] The United Nations Conference on Trade and Development (UNCTAD) was established in December 1964. Its role is to consider means for accelerating the economic development of less developed states through revised international trade policies.

[2] "The Dispute Settlement Machinery in the Convention on a Code of Conduct for Union Conferences," *Journal of Maritime Law and Commerce*, vol. 7, no. 1 (October 1975), p. 131.

[3] There are now about 360 conferences in the world; about 125 operate in U.S.

on Shipping Rings, reporting in 1907, investigated complaints by shippers and the public concerning the activities of shipping conferences, yet no fundamental changes in the U.K. law resulted and conferences remained unregulated.

In the United States, the House Merchant Marine Committee under Chairman Alexander began an investigation of conferences in 1912. Its report concluded that the established shipping lines plying foreign trade routes to and from American ports were parties to written agreements or gentlemen's understandings and, in many instances, were affiliated in shipping conferences. Among the techniques used to regulate competition, the conferences adopted pooling and price fixing. Percentage allotments based on prior carryings were established and profits of the pool were divided in accordance with those percentages. In addition there were territorial divisions of markets, restrictions of number of sailings and value of freight carried, and other devices to restrict or eliminate competition, all of which were deemed undesirable. Many of the recommendations of the Alexander Committee were drafted into the Shipping Act of 1916, representing the cornerstone of American regulatory policy in shipping. Conferences with open membership were accepted, provided they were fairly run. Many practices exposed by the Alexander Committee were prohibited, while others were to be strictly controlled by what is now the Federal Maritime Commission (FMC).

The major proponents of the shipping conferences do not deny the anticompetitive features of the conferences, but justify them on several grounds. They argue that conferences operate more efficiently than the competitive marketplace. Conferences can rationalize the trade, thus reducing rates to shippers. They also maintain orderly markets, avoid cutthroat price competition, maintain services to ports that otherwise would not receive them, and take a long-term view of interests of the trade.[4]

The frequent and often acrimonious disputes between the conferences and the major exporting countries, including the United States, caused the leading European shipping nations and Japan to form a loose governmental association in the early 1960s known as the Consultative Shipping Group (CSG). In a 1963 statement, the CSG ministers responsible for shipping concluded that the conference sys-

trades. Ronald A. Capone, "United States Laws and the Convention on a Code of Conduct for Liner Conferences: A Catalogue of Conflicts and Dilemmas," *Virginia Journal of International Law*, vol. 15, no. 2 (Winter 1975), p. 251.

[4] R. B. Farthing, "UNCTAD Code of Practice for the Regulation of Liner Conferences—Another View," *Journal of Maritime Law and Commerce*, vol. 4, no. 3 (April 1973), p. 467.

tem was indispensable but that a means should be provided to ensure fair practices and to provide a forum for discussing grievances of shippers. The ministers agreed with the shipowners that these should be provided by the conferences themselves rather than by governments.

In 1971 the ministers, meeting in Tokyo, confirmed the importance of the liner conferences, but at the same time laid down guidelines for the preparation of a code of conference practice. This code was to be a nongovernmental code, established jointly by the shippers councils in Europe and the conferences themselves. Based on these guidelines, the European and Japanese shipowners through their trade association CENSA and the European shippers councils negotiated a Code of Practice for Conferences in October 1971. This so-called CENSA code was viewed by members of the industry as a practical working document that emphasizes the discussion and conciliation processes outside of governmental channels.

Because the CENSA code was negotiated by the Europeans and Japanese without developing country input, it proved unacceptable to the LDCs. Therefore, at the 1972 United Nations Conference on Trade and Development in Santiago, Chile, the developing countries presented draft codes of conduct for negotiation at the governmental level.[5] Whereas the CENSA code defended the laissez faire structure, the LDCs wanted governments to regulate the conference system. Thus, UNCTAD adopted a resolution to begin work on a negotiated code.

The UNCTAD resolution was supported by a UN General Assembly resolution[6] passed over the objection of the maritime nations, including the United States. Subsequently, several preparatory sessions were held in 1973 leading up to an UNCTAD-convened plenipotentiary conference. Following lengthy negotiations, a detailed Code of Conduct for Liner Conferences (the Liner Code) emerged.[7]

The Liner Code, adopted on April 7, 1974, was supported by seventy-two nations. This support represented, generally, the less developed countries along with Australia, China, Japan, the Soviet bloc, Belgium, France, and Germany. Five developed countries (Can-

---

[5] This text resulted from Latin American and Afro-Asian drafts, which were unified. M. J. Shah, "The Dispute Settlement Machinery in the Convention on a Code of Conduct for Liner Conferences," *Journal of Maritime Law and Commerce*, vol. 7 (1975), p. 137.

[6] Resolution 3035, passed in December 1972.

[7] William J. Bosies, Jr., and William G. Green, "The Liner Conference Convention: Launching an International Regulatory Regime," *Law and Policy in International Business*, vol. 6 (1974), pp. 533–574; Capone, "Code of Conduct for Liner Conferences," pp. 249–276; and Shah, "Dispute Settlement Machinery," pp. 127–168.

ada, Greece, Italy, the Netherlands, and New Zealand) abstained from voting, and seven developed countries (the United States, Denmark, Finland, Norway, Sweden, Switzerland, and the United Kingdom) voted against the code. According to article 49, the code would go into effect "six months after the date on which not less than twenty-four States, the combined tonnage of which amounts to at least 25 percent of world [liner] tonnage, have become Contracting Parties to it. . . ."[8] If it has not entered into force within five years from the date of adoption of the final act of the United Nations Conference of Plenipotentiaries (April 1974), a review conference shall be convened at the request of one-third of the states entitled to become contracting parties to review the provisions therein and to consider amendments.

As of November 1978, only thirty-three nations, representing about 6 percent of the world liner tonnage, had ratified the code. No country with a significant fleet has yet become a party. The EEC countries debated a compromise to allow Germany, France, and Belgium to ratify the Liner Code, in spite of claims by others in the EEC that the code is inconsistent with the free-trade provisions of the Treaty of Rome. Nevertheless, in the event that enough of the shipping nations that voted for the code ratify it or a modified version of it restricted to developing country trade, the Liner Code could come into force.[9] It would then become the first UN-system negotiated multilateral code of conduct to regulate an international business activity.

Provisions

An evaluation of the Liner Code requires an understanding of the role of liner conferences in restricting competition and maximizing efficiency and profit. Chapter 1 of the UNCTAD Liner Code defines a liner conference as "a group of two or more vessel-operating carriers which provides international liner services for the carriage of cargo on a particular route or routes within specified geographical limits and which has an agreement or arrangement, whatever its na-

---

[8] Based on Lloyd's Register of Shipping, *Statistical Tables 1973*, as quoted in United Nations Conference on Trade and Development, *United Nations Conference of Plenipotentiaries on a Code of Conduct for Liner Conferences, Final Act and Annexes* (TD/Code/11/Rev. 1), May 9, 1974, p. 27.

[9] The LDCs, less flags of convenience states, account for 11.2 percent of world liner tonnage. The socialist Eastern bloc adds another 11.7 percent. The maritime powers voting for the code (France, West Germany, Japan, Liberia, Panama, and Singapore) amount to another 27.1 percent, more than enough to bring the code into effect. Capone, "Code of Conduct for Liner Conferences," p. 254.

ture, within the framework of which they operate under uniform or common freight rates and any other agreed conditions with respect to the provision of liner services." In U.S. trades, conferences must be open and may be joined by any carriers in the trade that meet certain reasonable criteria. In other trades, conferences may be closed and strictly limit membership; in addition many have internal commercial agreements to pool or share traffic or earnings. All conferences attempt to retain the greatest share of cargo movements on their routes for their own members. In U.S. trades, the Federal Maritime Commission must approve any pooling agreement that would result in a sharing of its traffic among the members of the conference.

The Liner Code contains 145 articles relating to conference membership, participation in trade, conference decision-making procedures, sanctions and self-policing, conference agreements, loyalty arrangements with shippers, publication of tariffs, consultation machinery, criteria for freight-rate determination (including surcharges and currency changes), adequacy of service, and machinery for the settlement of disputes. In other words, it contains detailed regulations about how conferences must be organized and operated. The most controversial of these subjects are conference membership, trade participation and cargo sharing, freight rate determination, and settlement of disputes.

Under article 1, any national shipping line has the right to be a full member of a conference that serves the foreign trade of its country whenever such a line is able to and intends to operate regular, adequate, and efficient service on a long-term basis. A national shipping line is defined by the code as a vessel-operating carrier that is recognized under the law of that country and that is headquartered in and under the control of that country. The U.S. Shipping Act of 1916 requires conferences serving the United States to admit all qualified carriers as equal members. Under the code a shipping line that is not a national line may be refused membership in a conference if the existing volume of trade, adequacy of shipping space, and probable effect of admission of the line do not warrant it. Under this provision, the Liner Code could perpetuate conference monopolies and the end result would be detrimental to commerce and the public interest.[10]

The code is also in conflict with section 14(a) of the Shipping Act of 1916, which authorizes the Federal Maritime Commission to determine cases in which any non-U.S. carrier serving U.S. trades is involved in an agreement to transport cargo between foreign ports.

---

[10] Ibid., p. 12.

If such an agreement excludes a U.S. citizen carrier from equal membership, the secretary of commerce may refuse the right of entry to the non-U.S. carrier.

The second major issue—trade participation and cargo sharing—was one of the most controversial addressed by the Liner Code negotiators. Article 2 stipulates that when conferences operate pools, shares of the trade must be allocated in such a way that national shipping lines of each trading partner carry equal shares of the bilateral trade while third-country shipping lines may acquire the remainder. Because pools are prohibited by U.S. law without prior approval on a case-by-case basis by the Federal Maritime Commission, this provision is in direct conflict with U.S. policy. Other paragraphs of article 2 permit automatically implemented or unilaterally imposed pooling arrangements by subgroups of conference lines. Article 2 (17) provides that trade participation applies to "all goods . . . with the exception of military equipment for national defense purposes." Although this clause conforms to U.S. law requiring defense shipments to be reserved in full to U.S. flag vessels, it conflicts with American law requiring all Export-Import Bank financed cargoes to be transported on U.S. carriers.[11] Other countries have similar laws requiring government and government-financed cargoes to be shipped on national flag vessels.

The Liner Code contains provisions for freight rate regulation. Article 12 states that "freight rates shall be fixed at as low a level as is feasible from the commercial point of view and shall permit a reasonable profit for shipowners. . . ." This article is consistent with the provision of the U.S. Shipping Act [section 18(b)(5)] which authorizes the FMC to determine whether a rate is either too high or too low, and therefore "detrimental to the commerce of the United States." Article 14 specifies that 150 days' prior notice be given for general rate increases, with a ten-month freeze between the previous increase and the next increase.[12] This fifteen-month freeze was felt to be too long by shipowners from all countries. Controversy also arose over articles 16 and 17. Article 16 provides that surcharges imposed by a conference for coverage of sudden or extraordinary increases in costs or losses of revenue shall be temporary; article 17 restricts rate adjustments due to changes in exchange rates.

---

[11] The relevant U.S. laws are: 10 U.S.C. 2631, requiring all defense cargoes to be carried by U.S. flag vessels; 15 U.S.C. 616(a), defining Export-Import Bank cargoes; and 46 U.S.C. 1241(b), reserving 50 percent for U.S. flag vessels.

[12] There is a disparity between the code and the Shipping Act of 1916, which prescribes a thirty-day notice, with a ninety-day notice in dual rate contract trades, and the right of conferences to increase rates at will.

The Liner Code provides shippers the right to receive certain information from shipping operators, such as information which could show predatory or cut-rate pricing, heretofore outlawed as a means of driving nonconference members out of business. Dual-rate contracts allowing discounts for shippers who commit themselves to ship with the conference are approved. And the formation of shippers councils to negotiate with conferences on an equal basis is encouraged.

The Liner Code's provisions for dispute settlement raise novel and far-reaching issues. Articles 23–46 detail the provisions and machinery available for settlement of disputes between a conference and a nonmember shipping line, the lines within a conference, a conference or shipping line and representatives of shippers, and two or more conferences. The conciliation procedures, outlined in full, apply to disputes relating to admission and expulsion from a conference, freight-rate increases, surcharges, currency adjustments, and inconsistencies of a conference agreement with the Liner Code. Article 30 proposes that an international panel of conciliators be established, composed of "experts of high repute or experience in the fields of law, economics of sea transport, or foreign trade and finance." The recommendation of the conciliators shall be binding by acceptance by the parties, unless they have agreed otherwise.

The Liner Code dictates that the disputes settled by mandatory conciliation take precedence over alternative solutions under national laws. This is a potentially far-reaching provision. Once accepted by the parties, the agreement shall be binding and all obligations imposed as if they were a final judgment by a court of that contracting party. Because the Shipping Act of 1916 gives the FMC authority to determine conference violations while the code grants precedence to the conciliation proceedings, there is a definite conflict between existing U.S. law and the Liner Code. Moreover, shipowners wish to retain familiar means of dispute settlement, a feeling shared by those from developed and developing countries alike.

Since the Liner Code's mandatory conciliation proceedings would take precedence over remedies available under national law, the proceedings would not be frustrated by parties invoking remedies under such laws as the U.S. Shipping Act and contract law. These remedies could include ordinary judicial processes, arbitration, conciliation initiated outside the Liner Code, and other means.

In an annex, the Liner Code provides model rules of procedure for international mandatory conciliation. In the absence of other procedures, the parties may agree to use these model rules. The developed countries argued against the mandating of specific rules of procedure, fearing that their rigidity would go against the spirit of conciliation. Most of the Group of Seventy-Seven in UNCTAD felt, however, that a body of rules was required to establish procedures that would secure and preserve the rights of the parties. The plenipotentiaries' conference finally decided against having mandatory rules, but proposed model rules in some detail. The Liner Code does not establish a system of regulation by an international entity. One of the objectives of almost all of the parties was to minimize the amount of institutional machinery required under the Liner Code. Although the conciliation machinery required some management, it was kept to a minimum. The secretary general of the United Nations was asked to appoint a registrar to maintain a list of conciliators, receive and maintain copies of requests for conciliation and ensuing documents, and make available information on completed cases.

The code does not sanction unilateral government action, nor does it even prescribe penalties for violation of its provisions. The Liner Code does, however, foresee that each contracting party will take legislative or other measures to implement the Liner Code. Therefore, the states that adopt the code can regulate by imposing penalties for violations. In addition, of course, governments may adopt the Liner Code as domestic law regardless of whether it comes into force as a multilateral convention.[13]

All activities encompassed by the Liner Code are, in fact, specifically regulated in U.S. trades by the Federal Maritime Commission under the Shipping Act. Rate setting and other agreements of conferences are required to be filed with the commission, and the commission may modify or disapprove such arrangements. Acts inconsistent with approved agreements are subject to penalties. To the extent anticompetitive agreements are deemed lawful under the Shipping Act, they are exempt from U.S. antitrust laws and their penalties.

Through the FMC and Department of Justice, the United States maintains that U.S. law can apply to agreements concluded outside its boundaries and by or with foreign carriers, because a state is entitled to take action in respect to activities initiated by anyone outside its borders that have consequences within its borders.[14] In theory, acquiring jurisdiction would not be an insurmountable difficulty because conference vessels call at and carry cargo to and from U.S. ports.

It is clear from these arrangements that the plenipotentiaries

---

[13] Capone, "Code of Conduct for Liner Conferences," p. 256.
[14] Ibid., p. 258.

agreed to minimize the role of international institutions in either the interpretation of the substantive provisions of the Liner Code or their enforcement. Great pains were taken during the negotiations to try to make the Liner Code as self-explanatory as possible. The self-contained conciliation procedure adopted in the Liner Code required only the intervention of a "house keeping" registrar for its implementation. Finally, the relations between shippers, shipowners, conferences, and government agencies were to be worked out on a case-by-case basis in each country or trade. The remedies provided by the Liner Code could be enforced in national courts but could not be frustrated by selective application of national laws.

In practice, however, conflicts of jurisdiction and perhaps even of national sovereignty would cause fundamental problems that may lead to confrontations. In those trades in which both Liner Code adherents and nonadherents are found, carriers and shippers will be forced into conflicts between the Liner Code or the laws of the non-adhering states. Two shipping regimes could exist side by side: that of those countries adhering to the code and that of those countries that do not. Unless potential conflicts between the two are resolved, "a world of regulatory chaos will exist for commercial interests."[15]

Impact

The Liner Code is the first international regulatory regime negotiated to achieve the particular objectives of the developing countries. The Liner Code would encourage LDCs to build up their own fleets and would eliminate some of the worst abuses of the conference system. With the new Liner Code, the developing countries have found an issue on which the developed countries could be split; several developed nations with large merchant fleets (Japan, France, Germany, and Belgium) have supported the Liner Code, probably in hope of increasing or maintaining their share of the trade with developing countries, while other traditional maritime countries including the United States have adamantly opposed the code.

The United States opposed the Liner Code because it is inconsistent with its own shipping laws, is anticompetitive, and puts significant and unnecessary restraints on vessel operators. The Liner Code would give conferences rights they do not now enjoy under U.S. law. Therefore, ratification of the Liner Code by the United States would imply a major change in U.S. regulatory philosophy.

The most troublesome aspect of the Liner Code for the United

---

[15] Ibid., p. 255.

States is its cargo-sharing provisions. As noted above, these provisions would divide a substantial proportion of the liner conference trade equally between ships of the two trading nations, reserving the remaining share to vessels of third countries (third-flag carriers). While no particular ratio is mandatory, if one trading partner does want a formula, it becomes compulsory between the two nations. A 40–40–20 formula, urged by the developing nations and included in early drafts of the code, is frequently cited and has become a benchmark.

The code's cargo-sharing provisions have been severely criticized as being in conflict with current U.S. policy and opposed to the interests of the United States and other nations. U.S. cargo preference law now requires at least 50 percent of all government-impelled cargoes to be transported on U.S. vessels, substantially more than that anticipated under the Liner Code. Further, potentially important sources of U.S. revenues derive from the operation of U.S. ships between foreign countries. This traffic would be threatened by the Liner Code's diminution of the role of third-flag carriers. The United Kingdom, Greece, and the Scandinavian nations would be even harder hit. Shipping lines in those states depend heavily on operations between foreign countries. According to one estimate, under a 40–40–20 formula European shipowners alone would lose $1.1 billion per year in revenues to developing country and Eastern bloc lines.

U.S. carriers have exhibited mixed reactions to the Liner Code's cargo-sharing provisions. Those carriers that service important routes between foreign countries have been fearful of the code's negative impact on third-flag carriers. Container operators that use feeder systems to marshal containers have been concerned lest they be considered third-flag carriers, and thus find their operations restricted. By contrast, some U.S. carriers have viewed cargo sharing as a possible remedy for their financial plight. The U.S. Department of Transportation has estimated that 40–40–20 sharing of traffic between the United States and its trading partners could increase annual U.S. carrier revenues by $500 million.[16] Further, cargo sharing in conjunction with closed conference operations would increase profit margins by enabling carriers to rationalize service by better using existing capacity and by planning for additional capacity.

But while the concept of cargo sharing has received some support among U.S. carriers, they are opposed to the universal implementation of any single formula (such as 40–40–20) to determine

---

[16] Robert Schuessler and David Spiller, "Report on the Economic Impacts of the UNCTAD Code of Conduct for Liner Conferences," U.S. Department of Transportation, 1975, pp. 4–5.

cargo shares. They prefer instead to negotiate bilateral cargo-sharing agreements, thus permitting U.S. carriers to exert more control over the allocation of cargo among states. Bilateral cargo-sharing arrangements were also preferred by the Department of Transportation study cited above. It found that cargo-sharing provisions do not necessarily benefit the U.S. merchant marine but that because of the growth of bilateral cargo-sharing agreements, such arrangements should be considered on a case-by-case basis.

Although U.S. flag operators have opposed American support of the Liner Code in its present form, they have been most concerned by the prospect of Liner Code coming into effect *without* U.S. adherence. One commentary has noted: "[W]idespread application of the Liner Code in the rest of the world could lead to extensive overtonnaging (and consequent rate warring) on U.S. trade routes, if third-flag carriers forced from non-U.S. trades gravitated to the less restrictive U.S. trades."[17] Because U.S. carriers operate high-cost, capital-intensive services, they are extremely vulnerable to declines in trade and rate cutting. Thus the fate of American carriers is inextricably linked to the fate of the Liner Code, whether or not the United States becomes a party to the code.

Most U.S. shippers fear that the anticompetitive nature of the Liner Code would result in poorer service and an inevitable increase in freight rates. Together, these circumstances could eventually produce a higher delivered cost on foreign trade commodities and, consequently, a decline in sales. Costs to shippers would rise if carriers were permitted to alter their schedules and port ranges. Should a shipper's regular port be removed from service or used with less regularity, additional problems and costs would arise from the need to reroute cargoes, to arrange inland transportation, to adjust inventory determination, to protect against pilferage and cargo damage, and to insure storage. The prospect of these costs and inconveniences has discouraged U.S. shippers from supporting the Liner Code.

The EEC nations have been seeking a common position on the Liner Code. The question they must resolve is the compatibility of the code with the Treaty of Rome, especially the treaty's provisions against discrimination. This could ultimately mean joint action by the nine EEC members with some or all acceding to the Liner Code or a modified version of it, thus virtually guaranteeing its adoption. Developing nations continue to urge that the Liner Code be adopted in its present form with the understanding that amendment could be made after the Liner Code enters into effect.

---

[17] Ibid., p. 10.

A number of Western shipping nations now believe that existence of some formula for cargo sharing is essential both for shipping relations with the developing countries and to counter the expansionist policies of Eastern bloc liner fleets. The Soviet Union now carries 70 percent of the total seaborne trade between itself and the EEC. Eastern bloc fleets have penetrated U.S. trades rapidly in recent years. Although they still carry only a small percentage of U.S. cargo, their rate cutting has attracted high-rated cargoes and has caused some rate wars. Eastern bloc fleets are faring so well in some cross trades that some observers feel the Soviet Union, which voted for the Liner Code, now has no real economic interest in seeing the Liner Code ratified.

Without the support of the Eastern bloc and some of the major developed maritime nations, the Liner Code cannot come into force. If that support is not forthcoming, then the Liner Code will remain a high-water mark of developing country diplomacy in UNCTAD, but with little or no practical effect on the world of shipping. Nevertheless, as the first such code to regulate an aspect of the international economy, it provides a precedent for all future similar efforts.

6

Code of Conduct on
the Transfer of Technology

Since the 1940s, economists have regarded technology as the organization of factors of production.[1] In this view, technology is not merely
one of the components of the development process (such as capital,
labor, machinery, and so on), but is rather the organization of all the
materials and inputs. While this broader view is helpful for understanding the development process, the codes and laws relating to the
transfer of technology usually deal only with the narrower view of
technology as embodied in patents, industrial know-how, and other
forms of application.

In this narrower sense, technology means the application of science to useful ends. Technology is the basis of modern industrial
society. In this century, developing countries have seen the explosion
of technology and their growing dependence on it, and they have
sought to change the terms and conditions under which they use
it. Hence, there is now a concern in both the developing and the
developed worlds about the conditions under which technology is
transferred.

Technology is property or, more precisely, it is possible to have
a property interest in technology. Thus the term "transfer of technology" is analogous to transfer of property. The fundamental dif-
ference is, of course, that if one transfers property such as a house
or an automobile, one no longer owns the property one has transferred. With technology, however, it is possible to transfer the rights
to use a patent, a technique, or any other embodiment of technology
and still be able to use it oneself. In other words, both the transferor
and the transferee may have property rights in the technology after

---

[1] P. N. Rosenstein-Rodan, "Problems of Industrialization of Eastern and South-
Eastern Europe," *The Economic Journal* (June-September 1943), pp. 202–211;
Colin Clark, *The Conditions of Economic Progress* (London: Macmillan, 1940).

the transfer. Perhaps a more appropriate term, therefore, would be "technology sharing," which describes the process and the result. On the other hand, the concept of technology as property (and concomitantly, payment for the right to use it) is important to retain; patent attorneys, licensing executives, and businessmen would probably quite rightly insist on it.[2]

A number of developing countries in the United Nations and other international organizations have called for the establishment of a code to regulate the transfer of technology.[3] As the UN's primary forum for developing country issues, UNCTAD has long had an interest in the effect of restrictive business practices on development. UNCTAD recommended in its first session in 1964 that the international community "explore possibilities for adoption of legislation concerning the transfer of industrial technology to developing countries, including the possibility of concluding appropriate international agreements in this field."[4] More recently at the UNCTAD conferences in Santiago (1972), Nairobi (1976), and Manila (1979), the transfer of technology from developed to developing countries was advocated as a major means of improving the developing countries' economic positions. And in the last year, negotiations on a Code on Restrictive Business Practices have been completed in UNCTAD, presaging the results of a Technology Code.

Developments outside UNCTAD

Several developing nations and one regional economic organization have adopted legislation regulating technology transfer. Although

---

[2] The term "technology transfer" has become widespread in the last few years. As most students of the subject have recognized, it is a very difficult term to define, as is technology itself. The Chamber of Commerce task force defined technology as involving "patents, designs, and technical data; it also includes the ability to put things together, to make things work to develop and satisfy customers, and to maintain efficient operations and uniform quality. Technology is also the desire—institutional and personal—that does not rest at any given level of achievement, but continually searches for improvement." Chamber of Commerce of the United States, *Technology Transfer and the Developing Countries* (Washington, D.C., April 1977), p. 3.

[3] For example, the UN Advisory Committee on Application of Science and Technology to Development in 1973 and the Fourth Conference of Heads of State or Government of Nonaligned Countries in September 1973 both issued such calls. In November 1974 the Latin American Conference on Industrialization similarly stated the need for an international code.

[4] United Nations, Conference on Trade and Development, *Proceedings of the U.N. Conference on Trade and Development, First Session* (Geneva, March 26–June 16, 1964), Vol. 1, Final Act and Report (E/Conf. 46/141/Vol. 1), 1964, annex A IV. 26 at 57, paragraph 3.

each country's legislation is somewhat different, the various laws offer a unique preview of the kinds of provisions likely to be included in whatever international agreement is ultimately drafted under UNCTAD auspices.

Under the Andean Code (Andean Common Market decision 24) discussed in chapter 4, all contracts dealing with the importation of technology, patents, and trademarks must be submitted for examination and approval to the government of the recipient. Contracts with provisions prohibited by the Andean Code are not to be authorized. Among these provisions are clauses that require the recipient to acquire products, raw materials, or technology from specific sources; clauses permitting the selling enterprise to fix the sale or resale prices of products manufactured under that technology; clauses that contain restrictions on volume or structure of production; clauses prohibiting the use of competitive technologies; clauses that establish a full or partial purchase option in favor of the supplier of the technology; clauses obligating the purchaser to transfer further improvements or inventions to the supplier; and other similar clauses. These provisions resemble laws now being adopted by other countries.

Mexico adopted rules regulating the transfer of technology in its patent and trademark laws and its contracts and agreements law. Mexico has long been a leader in the development of mechanisms to deal with the transfer of technology. The contracts and agreements law establishes standards by which foreign investment will be measured, comparing the investor's interest with the national interest. Its purpose is to screen out "dependency-creating" investments.[5] Although they are not gathered in one code, the registration requirements in Brazil are quite extensive and require the Directorate of Currency and Credit to register all foreign capital investment entering the country if patent or trademark rights covered by the agreement are being used in Brazil and are currently registered in both the country of origin and Brazil. Both the Mexican code and the Brazilian laws contain provisions invalidating contracts with restrictive clauses that limit the recipient country's right to export products using the transferred technology.[6] A similar law is in force in Argentina, and in

---

[5] Charles F. Schill, "The Mexican and Andean Investment Codes: An Overview and Comparison," *Law and Policy in International Business*, vol. 6 (1974), pp. 437, 475.

[6] United Nations Conference on Trade and Development, *Selected Principal Provisions in National Laws, Regulation, and Policy Guidelines* (TD/B/C.6/AC.1/2/ Supp. 1/Add. 1), 1975.

recognition of practical problems in applying it, greater flexibility has recently been given to its administrators.

In Europe, technology control laws exist in Spain and Portugal, the most recent being Portugal's decree-law 348/77 of August 24, 1977,[7] which defined a code for direct foreign investment. Joint agreements for the transfer of technology between residents in Portugal and residents abroad require special and prior authorization by the relevant authority. In such contracts, particularly between foreign firms and their branches in Portugal, clauses will not generally be permitted that tie technology to capital goods purchases, require the purchasers to transfer free any improvements, or restrict production or markets. Thus in both the developed and developing worlds, precedents for technology transfer regulation may be found.

The UNCTAD Negotiations

The impetus to develop international controls on technology transfer has not been lost within UNCTAD. If anything, these national and regional efforts have served to strengthen the resolve of UNCTAD members which have taken the lead in negotiations on a Technology Code.

In 1975, a Committee on Transfer of Technology was established as a main arm of the Trade and Development Board, the "manager" of UNCTAD. Concurrently, member governments agreed to begin work on a code of conduct for the transfer of technology, and a group of experts was established to that end. This group discussed a number of issues involving the transfer of technology, including the drafting of a code of conduct, the role of the patent system in technology transfer, and the assistance to be given by UNCTAD or other organizations to developing countries in negotiating technology transfer agreements.

One problem with these efforts is that few UNCTAD delegates participating in these decisions had any experience with the technical issues of intellectual property, research and development, or the needs of developing countries. Often, Geneva-based diplomats represent their governments on the basis of instructions cabled from their capitals and handle these issues along with many others. Some countries may send representatives from patent offices or intergovernmental relations offices of commerce or trade departments. Few

---

[7] Published in *Diario da Republica*, 1st series, no. 195, August 24, 1977.

delegations, other than that of the United States, have nongovernmental, legal, or industrial members.

At the fourth UNCTAD conference held in Nairobi in May 1976, the delegates agreed to begin negotiation of a technology code to be ratified within two years. Since there was no consensus on whether the code should be binding or voluntary, this issue was left open. A compromise was reached that provided that the code of conduct working groups recommend which parts should be mandatory and which should be voluntary. At this same conference, it was agreed that UNCTAD, as an organization, should participate in revising the 1885 Paris Convention on intellectual property.[8] It was also agreed that each country should have a "technology plan," should develop technological infrastructure, and should create regional and international institutions for the transfer of technology.

Two parallel drafts of a Code of Conduct for the Transfer of Technology (Technology Code) were proposed in the initial negotiations (see appendix B). The first was presented by the developing countries (the Group of Seventy-Seven at UNCTAD) in May 1975.[9] The developed countries responded with their own draft, and in February 1976 both groups presented revised drafts.[10] These texts represented the official submissions of governments and formed the basis for the ensuing negotiations.

Meetings of the Intergovernmental Group of Experts have been held since 1977 to try to iron out differences between the approaches embodied in the drafts, and to agree on a modus operandi. The method adopted by UNCTAD of working from drafts supplied by different groups has been criticized for heightening the confrontation between the developed and the developing countries. Critics also claim that it tends to lead to polarized positions rather than compromise solutions. Insufficient preparation by a secretariat with marked ideological biases in favor of the developing countries further hampers the work of the delegates. The approach used by UNCTAD committees and its secretariat should be contrasted with the more deliberate approach used

---

[8] The Paris Convention, negotiated in 1885, is currently being reviewed for possible revision and amendment by the World Intellectual Property Organization in Geneva.

[9] United Nations Conference on Trade and Development, *Report of the Intergovernmental Group of Experts on a Code of Conduct on Transfer of Technology* (TD/B/C.6/AC. 1/2), 1975.

[10] United Nations Conference on Trade and Development, *Report of the Intergovernmental Group of Experts on an International Code of Conduct on Transfer of Technology on its Third Session* (TD/AC. 1/9), 1977.

by the United Nations and the Centre for Transnational Corporations discussed in chapter 7.

Concepts of Technology Regulation

In the UNCTAD forum, as in all others, the developing countries argue strongly that there is an urgent need for the international regulation of large and wealthy multinational corporations. It is alleged that these organizations pose a real threat to the economic and political sovereignty of the developing countries. From a few specific cases, the developing countries argue for a universal, binding, and rigid code to define the rights and duties of corporations when contracting for the transfer of technology.

The Technology Code would have two major but separate functions. The first would be to establish an international agreement concerning restrictive business practices. Certain practices have long been considered anticompetitive by most developed countries, but few developing nations have prohibited them. Even in those countries that have, the prohibitions may not be completely or well enforced. It is in the U.S. interest to ensure the development in other countries of reasonable antitrust and procompetitive laws that do not, at the same time, unduly restrict the operations of U.S. multinational corporations.

The second function would be to encourage economic development through the modification of the terms and conditions under which technology is transferred between private parties. From the developing countries' point of view, agreements with foreign licensors often impose restrictions on use, increase foreign exchange drains, cause balance of payments problems, and increase costs to domestic firms. Therefore, they are prime candidates for regulation. LDCs also seek to increase the use of research and development conducted in their countries. These objectives can add to costs, increase administrative burdens, and reduce profits in already risky ventures. If, on top of this, national development planning is capricious or uncertain, then the multinational corporation faces ground rules that can be a continuing source of discontent and uncertainty.

Largely based on the experiences of Mexico and other Latin American nations, the developing countries have set out their objectives for the draft of the Technology Code. First, the code should be an international juridical regulatory scheme, worldwide in applicability. Second, the code should be arrived at by means of a treaty, establishing the fundamental principles governing the transfer of technology. Third, the code must be obligatory for the adhering states. Finally, UNCTAD must be the framework for the negotiations, which should be based on the preliminary draft of the Group of Seventy-Seven.[11]

The provisions of the Technology Code proposed in the draft of the Group of Seventy-Seven contain important concepts. These include:

- *National Regulations.* The draft foresees two parallel juridical lines: international legal regulations and national legal regulations. Measures that may be taken by states are outlined in the draft. The emphasis is admittedly on the regulation of the terms and conditions under which technology might be acquired.
- *Restrictive Commercial Practices.* The draft lists forty such practices and six types of cartels that might have adverse effects on technology transfers. The only practices considered illegal per se are those that are detrimental to the economy of the receiving country. This list went well beyond the elements contained in either the Mexican laws or the Andean Code.
- *Guarantees.* These provisions require, among other things, that the supplier warrant that the technology and equipment supplied are adequate for the aims of the contract and that they are being supplied at market prices. The required guarantees would be troublesome under the best of circumstances.
- *Special Treatment for Developing Countries.* This section includes proposals to establish institutions to improve the terms and conditions of transfer. This is argued by the Group of Seventy-Seven to be necessary to remove one of the major stumbling blocks to development.
- *International Cooperation.* A goal of the Group of Seventy-Seven is the exchange of information between countries, as well as the harmonization of national legislation on the subject of transfer of technology.[12]

It is in the area of requiring "appropriate technology" through guarantees that the Technology Code is perhaps on the shakiest conceptual ground. The draft contained a long list of provisions that must be guaranteed by the suppliers of the technology.[13] The provisions require that the technology be suitable and appropriate for the

---

[11] Jaime Alvarez Soberanis, "The Need for the Formation of an International Code of Conduct for the Transfer of Technology," Council of the Americas, New York (1977), pp. 31–34.

[12] Ibid., pp. 29–34.

[13] United Nations Conference on Trade and Development, *Report of the Intergovernmental Group of Experts on a Code of Conduct on Transfer of Technology on its Resumed Session* (TD/B/C. 6/14), 1976.

needs and capabilities of the recipient, that a minimal level of production be achieved, and that local inputs and consultants be used in selecting the technology. Further, the draft requires that national personnel be adequately trained to use the technology transferred, the recipient have access to all improvements, the recipient acquire required capital goods and inputs from the supplier at prices no higher than current international levels, and more favorable terms granted to any other recipient be extended to subsequent recipients in similar positions within the same country.

It is hard to imagine what standards, mechanisms, and institutions would have to be developed to fully implement these rules. On the one hand, the rules seem to require the foreign transferor to guarantee certain technologies in its agreements. On the other hand, they imply that these guarantees will be monitored and challenged by government authorities. At minimum, the rules seem to imply some right to monetary recourse on the part of the recipient company, if not the recipient country, for noncompliance by the multinational corporation. If the details of the implementation of these momentous provisions are left to national law, little harmony will result.

UNCTAD has recognized the institutional deficiencies of the LDCs as technology recipients, particularly in dealing with the question of appropriate technology. It has suggested the establishment of national and regional centers for the transfer of technology.[14] These centers would identify technological needs; collect, store, and distribute information on alternative technologies; and evaluate and select appropriate technologies for the needs of each developing country.[15] It is evident that many developing countries will not have the expertise available within the country, particularly within governmental sectors, to deal in an intelligent way with many of the complex issues involved in selecting appropriate technologies. They may have better luck, however, dealing with some of the issues surrounding restrictive business practices, terms and conditions of licensing, and other transfer arrangements.

The draft prepared by the developing countries contained a provision that each government may establish or strengthen mechanisms

---

[14] United Nations Conference on Trade and Development, *Establishment of Centres for the Transfer and Development of Technology* (TD/B/c. 6/9/Add. 3), 1975, as quoted in Countess Pease Jeffries, "Regulation of Transfer of Technology: An Evaluation of the UNCTAD Code of Conduct," *Harvard International Law Journal*, vol. 18, no. 2 (Spring 1977), p. 311.

[15] This effort is paralleled in the UN Industrial Development Organization's proposed Industrial and Technological Information Bank and by the UN Commission on Transnational Corporations, which is discussing the provision of technical assistance to LDCs in economic, legal, and financial areas.

in administrative systems for proper enforcement of the rights and obligations flowing from the technology transfer transactions.[16] This is the only provision in the draft dealing with enforcement mechanisms. In the examples given above of developing countries (Mexico and Brazil) as well as the one regional economic organization (the Andean Common Market), enforcement provisions have proved to be diverse in substance and uneven in applicability. This would certainly not portend uniformity of enforcement or simplicity of multinational operations.

Specific Issues

It is against this background and these conceptual bases that government negotiators must deal with provisions to be included in a Technology Code. Both the Group of Seventy-Seven and the Group B (developed nations) drafts address the question of restrictive business practices. Both contain lists of clauses and practices considered to be restrictive. As may be expected, the LDC list is more extensive and detailed than the Group B list. The LDC list of restrictive business practices that would be prohibited includes

- restrictions on the recipient's volume, scope, or range of production
- restrictions on obtaining competing or complementary technology through patents and know-how from other sources, or restrictions on the sale or manufacture of competing products
- limitations by the supplier regarding the source of supply of raw materials, spare parts, and capital goods
- limitations on the diffusion and further use of technology already available, and on requiring additional payments for repeated use of the same technology.

One of the standards by which to judge the provisions of a technology code is U.S. competition and antitrust law. Under U.S. antitrust law, certain of the proposals in the Group of Seventy-Seven draft are not only acceptable but desirable. In those areas where "traditional" restrictive business practices have been dealt with, the United States should have no objection. These would include restrictions on exports, unreasonable restrictions on field of use, collection of royalties on expired patents, and the exercise of excessive market power.

By the fourth session of the expert group in February 1978, there

---

[16] United Nations Conference on Trade and Development, *Report of the Intergovernmental Group of Experts on a Code of Conduct on Transfer of Technology on its Resumed Session*, annex II, paragraph 3.2 (xi).

were some fourteen provisions on which genuine differences of approach between Group B and the Group of Seventy-Seven existed.[17] These perhaps represented the real conceptual differences between the two groups. The most important of these include the following:

- The Group of Seventy-Seven would like to see all restrictions on the transferee end at the expiration of a licensing or technology transfer arrangement. This stems from its philosophy that technology must be "sold," not leased or rented. The developed nations in Group B, on the other hand, felt that the parties must be able to contract for whatever deal makes sense, and if this involves restrictions beyond the life of a patent, so be it.
- The Group of Seventy-Seven would like to "unbundle" know-how from patents so that if the latter are invalidated or expire, then no payments for them and the associated know-how would be made. Group B felt that in many cases it is impossible to unbundle or disentangle the two elements and that there should be no provision in the agreement requiring unbundling.
- The Group of Seventy-Seven would like to preserve the right of the licensee to challenge the validity of the patents. Group B suggested that the licensor may terminate the license if in fact the licensee challenges the patent's validity, but he may not prevent the licensee from making such a challenge.
- The Group of Seventy-Seven would not like to see contractual restrictions placed either on research or on use of personnel. Group B felt that these kinds of controls are managerial and will avoid duplication in subsidiaries and affiliates. Furthermore, the question of how long it would take for a licensee to "reverse engineer" a product or analyze a substance to determine its components would not then be an issue.

In addition to these traditional business practice problems, the Group of Seventy-Seven has introduced new concepts: the question of the licensor's warranties to the licensee, the relations between subsidiaries and parents, and the choice of tribunal. The warranty problem involves, as previously noted, the introduction of guarantees not only of completeness but also of fitness and suitability. Licensors tend to avoid these kinds of warranties even in dealing with affiliates in developed countries, to say nothing of wishing to avoid responsibility for production or processes being installed in distant countries, perhaps even by untrained personnel. Obviously, the more qualitative

---

[17] Joel Davidow of the Antitrust Division of the U.S. Department of Justice, at ABA Conference on Restrictive Business Practices and International Transfer of Technology, New York, December 14, 1977.

aspects of technology, such as its suitability or appropriateness, could lead to disputes not only with the licensee but with the licensee's government.

The Group of Seventy-Seven's draft code suggests that only host country tribunals may settle disputes under the code between licensee and licensor. In addition to its obvious one-sidedness, such a provision flies in the face of developments in many other forums for dispute settlement, including the intergovernmental forums of the International Finance Corporation, the Organization of American States, the Inter-American Convention on International Commercial Arbitration, the UN Commission on International Trade Law rules, and the private forums of the International Chamber of Commerce and similar organizations. The Group of Seventy-Seven draft also incorporates the Calvo Doctrine, limiting the intervention of home governments of multinational firms in their disputes with host governments.[18] Moreover, this proposal by the Group of Seventy-Seven elevates the Calvo Doctrine to a level of pure abstraction in the international community at a time when the developing countries seem to be more practical on a national level. To be more precise, certain Latin American countries espousing the Calvo Doctrine have nevertheless accepted U.S. government intervention in investment disputes. In many countries, subrogation of rights to the United States through the U.S. Overseas Private Investment Corporation is now accepted; the code would prohibit such subrogation.

The Group of Seventy-Seven draft introduced the issue of the relationship between parents and subsidiaries as potentially involving restrictive practices. The proposed code is generally concerned with the freedom of subsidiaries and many of its provisions would interfere with the management of subsidiaries by their parents. For example, payments from subsidiaries to parents would be regulated. There is also an insistence in the Group of Seventy-Seven draft that subsidiaries have the ability or potential to compete with their parents.

These provisions would not encourage the free flow of investment or the transfer of the latest and best technology to subsidiaries. Indeed, these provisions in particular could subvert the major objective of the developing countries, development through technology

---

[18] The Calvo Doctrine holds that questions of compensation for expropriated or nationalized property should be settled in accordance with national laws applied by the expropriating state dealing directly with the former property owner without intervention of the home government of the expropriated company. While this doctrine has not been observed vigorously in the past, its inclusion and explicit approval in the code further shifts the balance in the direction of the expropriating state.

transfers. Obviously one of the reasons multinational corporations include such restrictions is to prevent competition from their licensees in other markets. The elimination of those restrictions will force the licensor to weigh the advantages of a particular license with loss of other markets. The result may be a decision to license at much higher prices or not at all. Perhaps by adopting more flexible language in the Technology Code, national governments could be given the latitude to review the particular circumstances of any given arrangement, permitting those restrictive clauses that have no adverse effect on the national economy or the national interest of the recipient company host nation.

The Group of Seventy-Seven draft also provides that governments may define the price and specify levels and modalities of payments.[19] This suggests that it is possible to isolate and define the various components of the typical kinds of arrangements made between licensees and licensors, between parents and subsidiaries, or between joint venturers. Such a task is at best difficult, at worst impossible.

Impact

Without question, the Technology Code would place awesome new demands upon both multinational corporations and host governments, taxing their resources and capabilities. Government bureaucracies would be required to register, screen, and perhaps approve technology transfer agreements, requiring agencies staffed with knowledgeable personnel. It is unlikely, though, that scarce, technically qualified personnel could be bid away by government agencies from the private sector. Information would have to be provided by both the sellers and buyers of technology, not only on the deal itself, but also on all operations, to establish reasonable standards for costs and profits. Negotiations have not indicated how governments can define prices of technology. In order to prevent discouragement of investment, not only must the cost of factors of production (including capital) be met, but a profit margin must also be included. This seems to lead in the direction of standards for calculating costs and perhaps even profits. Such issues are not yet handled uniformly well within the United States, much less within countries with such diverse sociological, market, and historical backgrounds as those negotiating the Technology Code.

---

[19] United Nations Conference on Trade and Development, *Report of the Intergovernmental Group of Experts on a Code of Conduct on Transfer of Technology on its Resumed Session*, paragraph 3.2 (x), as quoted in Jeffries, "Regulation of Transfer of Technology," p. 310.

Another obstacle is that the Technology Code would leave the details of legislation up to each member country. While drafting in this manner gives greater flexibility, it does not lead to uniformity of international standards. Seen in its worst light, the Technology Code would only serve to legitimize unilateral efforts, which might be quite divergent in impact and effect. Thus one purpose of negotiating any code of conduct—to achieve international uniformity and to increase harmony among national laws—would be defeated. As a result, multinationals would face a variety of interpretations and may continue to channel investments to those countries offering the most favorable investment climates.

The question of the legal form of the Technology Code may or may not be important. It may be important if there is sufficient consensus on the final text that not only the developing countries but also the developed capital and technology exporters feel it is an important, workable document. In that case an argument could be made that a "good" code should be binding on all nation signatories, and that such a code would be in the interest of the United States.

Efforts within UNCTAD to develop a Technology Code have not gone unnoticed by the American business community. In an attempt to forestall drastic changes in the current system of technology transfer and to present a more liberal economic perspective on the issue, the U.S. Chamber of Commerce Task Force on Technology Transfer published a report in April 1977 that urges the creation of a favorable environment for the transfer of technology and discourages measures that can only impair the process. Although the document does not purport to be an official policy position of the chamber, it clearly represents the views of many members of the U.S. business community.

The report begins by observing that technology transfer is a continuing and voluntary process; transfer can be forbidden or discouraged, but it cannot be compelled. The chamber report notes that the proposed UNCTAD Code of Conduct for the Transfer of Technology is only partly a list of dos and don'ts for companies. Primarily it is a mandate for the governments of technology importing countries to overturn existing arrangements, legal and contractual, in the belief that independence from foreign technology may be achieved.[20] That sovereign countries can restructure their legal environments is taken for granted; that they can do so and, at the same time, strengthen their technology and close the development gap seems improbable.

The Chamber task force makes a number of suggestions for serious consideration by the United States and foreign governments:

---

[20] Chamber of Commerce of the United States, *Technology Transfer*, p. 14.

- The U.S. government should undertake a campaign of education concerning the potentials of technology transfer for economic development and the danger of disincentives. Educational exchanges, technical assistance, and similar arrangements should be undertaken. At the same time, business executives, industrial managers, and others should initiate dialogues through conferences and informal communications to share thoughts and experience.
- The U.S. government should continue to encourage the establishment of research and development institutions, and to aid national and regional development banks.
- Although the government should not adopt a "Hickenlooper Amendment"[21] for industrial property, the report does suggest that the U.S. government should recognize and act on the principle that technology constitutes a property interest entitled to protection.
- The U.S. government should consider encouraging the exchange of technology through incentives such as tax deferrals or credits, or a system of insurance, to firms transferring technology to affiliated transferees in developing countries. Such arrangements would be available to developing countries that refrain from arbitrary action in derogation of existing agreements, agree to arbitration for dispute settlement, and agree not to put unreasonable restrictions on access to their technology and markets.
- Disincentives for breaches of technology agreements should also be considered by the United States. These could include denying entry into the United States of products manufactured by the use of such technology. The chamber urges the use of existing arrangements and mechanisms for arbitrating disputes, and suggests that such agreements to arbitrate not be upset by short-sighted and self-defeating nationalism.
- Finally, the chamber urges that UNCTAD avoid an open split between those who have and those who need technology by precipitating premature adoption of a "code of conduct" at variance with facts and principles set forth in the chamber policy statement. The chamber concludes that the U.S. government should provide leadership to improve the conditions for technology transfer, to protect technology already in place from improper ap-

---

[21] The Hickenlooper Amendment, adopted in 1962, would suspend U.S. foreign aid if a country nationalized or expropriated property of a U.S. citizen, without discharging its obligations under international law for compensation. In 1973 the amendment was modified to permit the president to waive its application on national interest grounds. Ibid., p. 21.

propriation, and to work to clear the atmosphere of suspicion that threatens the development process itself.

Conclusions

The draft Technology Code produced by the developing countries and other UNCTAD documents display little or no concern for the underlying premises in favor of competition on which American and European doctrines of restrictive business practices rest. Further, those U.S. doctrines developed on a case-by-case basis allow scope for inquiry into particular business or economic circumstances, the bargaining power of the parties, and the competition to be protected. Unless these kinds of factors may be taken into account, the code is too blunt an instrument.

Tying clauses compelling licensees to purchase unpatented goods from the licensor cannot stand in American law, and they should not be permitted in international commerce. In contrast, however, other restraints may well make legal and economic sense and should not be prohibited outright. Host governments should be prepared to evaluate justifications offered in favor of such arrangements on their merits. This is particularly important where codes or laws might be interpreted by relatively inexperienced or junior bureaucrats who do not have the power to vary from the terms of the law. Thus a "rule of reason" is certainly appropriate to ensure that neither the transferor nor the transferee be entitled to abuse his position of power.

7

Code of Conduct
for Transnational Corporations

Multinational corporations have had a dramatic impact on international economics and have tended to accentuate interdependency among nations. The size and geographical reach of multinational corporations, as well as their growing control of major world resources, have caused increasing political concern. Many of the ills suffered by developing countries have been attributed to the socioeconomic system that fosters corporations that are private, independent, and multinational. Thus, mass poverty, unemployment, inflation, political injustice, corruption, deterioration of the human environment, and racism have all been laid at the multinational corporation's door.

Although pressures against multinational corporations had been building through the 1960s, generalized theoretical objections such as these may never have triggered concerted international action toward a code of conduct were it not for one political act—the stirring and articulate protest by the Chilean representative to the United Nations against interference by ITT in his country's internal political affairs. Largely in response to that protest, the United Nations in 1972 created the Group of Eminent Persons to examine and report on the activities of multinational corporations.[1] In UN Economic and Social Council Resolution 1721 setting up the group, both the positive and negative aspects of multinational corporations were recognized, but the overwhelming attitude was one of condemnation.[2]

Even before the report of the eminent persons was published,

---

[1] The Group of Eminent Persons was appointed by the secretary general in July 1972 to study the role of transnational corporations and their impact on economic development. Resolution 1721 (LIII).

[2] Nian T. Wang, "The Design of an International Code of Conduct for Transnational Corporations," *Journal of International Law and Economics*, vol. 10 (1975), pp. 319–320.

proposals for an international code for multinational corporations were made in 1973 by the UN Secretariat in a report titled *Multinational Corporations in World Development*.[3] The secretariat suggested negotiation of such a code as part of the work program of the Economic and Social Council. When the eminent persons' report was issued the following year, it, too, recommended that the international community develop a code of conduct for transnational corporations. Its concept of a code was a set of recommendations that would gradually evolve and reflect experience and changing circumstances. The group stressed that the code it recommended would not be compulsory in character but rather would be an instrument of moral persuasion strengthened by the authority of international organizations and the support of public opinion.[4]

Several other developments also occurred in 1974 to give focus to the debate. Secretary of State Kissinger proposed that the United States and Latin America jointly develop principles that would govern the behavior of transnational corporations.[5] Work was also undertaken at the OECD on a code of conduct for multinationals (see chapter 4). Further impetus to the concept of a code of conduct was given by the UN General Assembly's passage of the resolution on a New International Economic Order (NIEO). Paragraph 4 of that resolution included a call for regulation and supervision of the activities of transnational corporations by taking measures in the interest of the national economies of the host countries.[6] In the parallel program of action[7] adopted by the United Nations, under the heading of regulation and control over the activities of transnational corporations, the formulation of a Code of Conduct for Transnational Corporations was strongly endorsed. It was clear that the objective was to prevent interference by corporations in the internal affairs of host countries, to eliminate collaboration with racist regimes, to regulate business practices, and to ensure conformity of corporation activities with national development plans. To be effective, the code would have to deal with the transfer of technology as well as with the issues of rates of profits and reinvestment. By these General Assembly resolutions, the United Nations went on record as clearly opposing the further development

---

[3] UN Document ST/CA 190, 1973.

[4] United Nations Economic and Social Council, *The Impact of Multinational Corporations on Development and on International Relations* (E/5500/Rev. 1/ ST/ESA/6), 1974, p. 55.

[5] Statement to the Fourth Regular General Assembly of the OAS on April 20, 1974, in *Department of State Bulletin*, vol. 70 (1974), pp. 510–511.

[6] Resolution 3201 (S-VI), 1974.

[7] General Assembly Resolution 3202 (S-VI).

of transnational corporations without some form of international regulation.

The Charter of Economic Rights and Duties of States, adopted by the General Assembly in 1974[8] as a companion to the NIEO, emphasized the importance of the effort. In article 1, the charter reaffirms the right of states to exercise sovereignty over national resources. Article 2 declares that every state is entitled to regulate foreign investment in accordance with "its laws and regulations and in conformity with its national objectives and priorities." Furthermore, the charter declares that each state is entitled to expropriate ownership of foreign property with appropriate compensation "taking into account *its* relevant laws and regulations and all circumstances that *the State considers pertinent*" (emphasis added). The charter goes on to say that where controversies arise over compensation, they will be settled under the domestic laws of the nationalizing state and by its tribunals unless it is agreed otherwise.[9]

To give some practical effect to these resolutions and statements urging control of multinationals, the UN Commission on Transnational Corporations was established by resolution 1913 (LVII) of the United Nations Economic and Social Council in December 1974. The commission is composed of forty-eight members elected by the council for three-year terms.[10] The commission was given the task of formulating a universal standard or "code of conduct" for transnational companies, combining national policies with international interests. The commission is also to provide (1) a comprehensive review of transnational corporations, (2) a forum for exchange of views between interested governmental and nongovernmental groups, (3) an advisory service for the UN Centre on Transnational Corporations, (4) a research organization on activities of transnational corporations, and (5) a consultative group to the Economic and Social Council.

At the first session of the Commission on Transnational Corporations in March 1975, members presented varying views and proposals for its work program. At its second session in Lima, Peru, in March 1976, the commission gave highest priority to the formulation of a Code of Conduct for Transnational Corporations (the Transnational Code), and delegated an Intergovernmental Working Group to finalize a draft code by the spring of 1978. All countries were asked to

---

[8] Resolution 3281 (XXIX).

[9] The effect of these provisions is to further institutionalize the Calvo Doctrine (see chapter 6, note 18).

[10] Geographical distribution includes twelve from Africa; eleven from Asia; ten from Latin America; ten from Western Europe, North America, and Oceania; and five from the socialist states of Eastern Europe.

present their views on the code, and the UN Centre[11] was instructed to bring together these governmental proposals in a single document. A second working group was appointed by the secretary general to set standards of accounting and reporting for transnational corporations, and a third working group was proposed for the purpose of negotiating a multilateral agreement on corrupt practices, particularly illicit bribery, in international commercial transactions.[12]

The Working Group on the Code of Conduct and the UN Centre for Transnational Corporations have taken a deliberate and systematic approach to developing the Transnational Code. Working documents have been prepared by the secretariat discussing the issues involved in drafting the code, and the views of various states and nongovernmental organizations on these issues have been sought. A number of basic issues were discussed in these early reports, including the scope of the code, its legal nature, the subjects that should be regulated, and enforcement mechanisms.

Nevertheless, the trend of the effort has become clear. From the working group's January 1977 session has come an annotated outline of a Transnational Code that finesses many of these issues; those that are not finessed are decided against the multinational corporations. The outline covers issues identified by the Centre on Transnational Corporations;[13] the provisions largely embody the conclusions reached on the issues by the secretariat. Even though the chairman suggested that the outline should be considered neutral and descriptive and "not include formulations of a legal, normative, or imperative character," every provision presumes past guilt of transnational corporations.[14]

As one prominent example, in a section on noninterference in

---

[11] The Centre on Transnational Corporations was formed as an autonomous part of the United Nations Secretariat and began to function in November 1975. It is a research and support group to both the UN Commission on Transnational Corporations and the UN Economic and Social Council. It is gathering and analyzing information for the development of a code of conduct, while at the same time providing technical advice to governments in a coordinated manner.

[12] The Ad Hoc Working Group on the Problem of Corrupt Practices adopted an annotated outline as a basis for its work and has initiated discussion over the formal language an international agreement may contain. The major points of dispute involve the adoption of an international agreement as opposed to unilateral measures which reflect the specific situation of each nation. Some members preferred to focus only on bribery in international commercial transactions; others preferred a broader scope.

[13] United Nations Centre on Transnational Corporations, *Transnational Corporations: Issues Involved in the Formulation of a Code of Conduct* (E/C. 10/17).

[14] United Nations General Assembly, *Work Related to the Formulation of a Code of Conduct: Report of the Intergovernmental Working Group on a Code of Conduct* (E/C. 10/31), May 4, 1977.

governmental relations, one finds the language: "abstention by transnational corporations from requesting their home governments to exert pressure on host governments beyond normal diplomatic representation." This formulation presupposes that not only have multinationals exerted such pressure on host governments in the past, but that this practice is wrong and should be outlawed. Neither conclusion was justified on the basis of the evidence or the decisions before the commission. Such a formulation puts the Transnational Code clearly on the side of expropriating countries in their continuing contest with expropriated companies.

Issues in the Transnational Code

The staff of the Centre on Transnational Corporations believes that one of the functions of the Transnational Code is to build upon, and perhaps incorporate, much more specific and detailed regulatory work going on elsewhere. Under the outline's sections on taxation, restrictive business practices, transfer of technology, employment, and environmental protection, the draft suggested that "account is to be taken" of work being done elsewhere. Precisely what form this "account" might take is open to question. Does it mean the Transnational Code would supersede the work of the International Labor Organization, UNCTAD, the UN Group on Tax Treaties, the UN Environmental Program, or other groups? Does this mean the adoption of conflicting provisions in different international codes? Perhaps most importantly, does it mean the Transnational Code is to make legally binding provisions that are now being negotiated elsewhere as guidelines in voluntary form, such as UNCTAD's "voluntary" guidelines on restrictive business practices, a code under discussion since 1974?

It is clearly the intention of the drafters of both the issues paper and the annotated outline to be as comprehensive and inclusive as possible. Thus, the annotated outline deals with political issues as well as with a wide variety of economic, financial, and social issues. In the view of some observers, this approach almost certainly dooms the effort to failure. It is much more likely that agreement can be reached on only a few specific substantive areas, even at the leisurely pace of such negotiations.[15] In this view, a code could be built up over time by a process of accretion. Two areas that may be ripe for such agreement are restrictive business practices and transfer pricing, but these are only two of dozens of topics incorporated in the draft outline.

[15] Seymour J. Rubin, "Harmonization of Rules: A Perspective on the United Nations Commission on Transnational Corporations," *Law and Policy in International Business*, vol. 8 (1976), p. 888.

Conceptually, the most fundamental demand behind the Transnational Code is that multinational firms adhere to the economic goals and development objectives of states. This general concept could support a series of specific provisions such as that contained in the annotated outline calling for a "renegotiability of contracts to which transnational corporations are parties, in connection with national development plans and regional integration arrangements." This would suggest that only one side to a contract regarding a mineral concession or an investment program is bound by it; any host state, depending upon its own economic, long-term, or even momentary political needs, could demand the renegotiation of contracts under the guise of a "development plan."[16]

Because such provisions have been included in the draft, some delegations have found it necessary to urge that multinational corporations be treated equitably by all governments in accordance with international law, especially with respect to nationalization and provision of compensation. Other delegations, conversely, have defended such provisions as rightful extensions of national sovereignty by states over their economies and natural resources. They have further asserted that such provisions are a just preference to developing countries.[17]

Another example of a troublesome provision can be found under the section dealing with balance of payments. The outline provides that multinational corporations might be obliged to refrain from repatriating capital or remitting profits, royalties, or fees if such transfers would cause balance-of-payments difficulties. In this, the multinational firm is in danger of being made a scapegoat for, and at the mercy of, every country's unfavorable balance of payments. A multinational corporation's concern with its continued ability to get its profits and investment out of the host country would be accentuated by such a provision. This could only adversely affect future decisions to invest abroad. Concern would be most acute in those less developed countries with few export commodities that necessarily experience the most serious balance-of-payments problems. Yet these are the very countries with the greatest need for new investment.

The draft Transnational Code could lay the groundwork for

---

[16] As one experienced observer notes, "Many developing nations do not view rules of law against restrictive business practices as neutral instruments to promote the greatest possible economic competition, but as shields to protect their struggling economies from domination by the transnational enterprises of the developed nations." Mark R. Joelson, "The Proposed International Codes of Conduct as Related to Restrictive Business Practices," *Law and Policy in International Business*, vol. 8 (1976), p. 847.

[17] UN Centre on Transnational Corporations, *The CTC Reporter*, vol. 1, no. 2 (June 1977), p. 12.

further significant discrimination in national law against multinational corporations. A draft provision requires such firms to provide relevant information on transfer prices and intragroup pricing policies to government authorities. Certainly government authorities would have to interpret the requirement and the relevance of information requested, but the concept of transfer and intragroup pricing is vague enough to justify very broad requests. Thus transnational corporations might be forced to provide much more information than their local competitors under dubious assurances of confidentiality. A similar provision is proposed under the section on taxation, with an even broader requirement—"relevant information for tax purposes"—that could conceivably cover almost any information request. In the section on competition and restrictive business practices, it is proposed that the Transnational Code deal with "anticompetitive behavior by transnational corporations by abusing dominant market positions." A requirement is placed on multinationals, but not domestic corporations, to adhere to the Transnational Code's standards, whatever they may finally turn out to be.

The participation of host governments in the process of technology transfer is explicitly sanctioned. As in the Andean Code, it is clear that host governments expect to be considered "third-party beneficiaries," with an interest in the contract between transferor and transferee. If the Transnational Code requires the submission of agreements to government authorities for approval (as is already the case in countries such as Mexico, Argentina, Brazil, Portugal, and the Andean Pact countries), the basis will exist for control of the substantive provisions of all know-how, patent, and trademark licensing arrangements, and the remittances deriving from them. Multinational firms will no doubt be required to contribute to the scientific and technical development of their host countries, in ways that are not now specified.

Lastly, a potentially troublesome provision would require that multinational firms supply information to affiliates and subsidiaries regarding such matters as taxation, exports, imports, transfer pricing, contribution to development objectives, and restrictive business practices. A similar provision is proposed with respect to disclosure of information to employees. Again a distinction would be drawn between multinational and domestic firms; the obvious discrimination against the former will make employee groups and labor unions much more potent in actions against them than against domestic firms. These provisions could also be used by governments to shift the bargaining power in favor of the host country subsidiaries. The annotated outline's general concern about multinational leverage and host country development raises the possibility that provisions having that effect might be included.

As the elaboration of the Transnational Code proceeds, governments will have to pay close attention, not only to the problems discussed here, but many others. The conceptual basis of the code will have to be reexamined continually, the evidence sifted, and the language tested against reality. The United States, in particular, as the home of so many of the multinationals which are the subject of the code, has a special interest and its views are, and should be, of greater weight than most other countries. It is toward the development of those views that the final chapter is presented.

8

Toward the Development of a U.S. Position

Various options can be identified for future U.S. policy with respect to the codes described in this work and any that follow. Because this is not a position paper prepared for a specific negotiation, and given the wide variety of problems encountered, a certain simplification and exaggeration in the statement of options are inevitable.

At the extreme, there are three general attitudes that the United States may adopt in dealing with the international negotiation of codes of conduct. The first policy would call on the United States to embrace the codes and do all in its power to bring them into force as legally binding international agreements. Our justification would be that codes are needed as international business becomes more widespread and complex. The objectives of the codes are worthy; they express the best of the international community's thinking on these issues; and, in many cases, they bring legislation and regulations throughout the world into line with U.S. laws and practices. We cannot legitimately object to codes that in some instances only reflect U.S. domestic law. If the codes are not perfect, they are at least more workable than the alternatives and better than no agreement on these real issues. They can be effective regulatory devices.

A second position would be to accept codes skeptically, with reservations. We would recognize that most codes are too ambitious in scope, overly infected by the twin vices of theoretical economics and the political rhetoric of developing countries. Although codes in general might be inconsistent with U.S. free-enterprise ideals, this should not blind us to those operative provisions that on balance are reasonable and just (or can be made so). We would recognize that if codes are properly drawn with our help, they will work in practice and can be significant steps in the right direction in achieving global understanding. The risk is small since, if their terms are not acceptable, we could work to minimize their impact.

The third alternative would be to oppose codes in any and all forms, but most especially the legally binding codes with enforceable provisions. We could reluctantly accept guidelines or the more general codes, such as that of the OECD, but binding codes would be seen as undesirable forms of control over private enterprise, imposed by groups of developing countries largely for political reasons. Binding codes would, inevitably, regulate international affairs to the detriment of multinational corporations and enterprises of all types from developed countries. They are thus viewed as unwarranted interference with the terms and conditions of private contracts and transactions that will "rig the game" against corporations from developed countries. Rights of private property will be further eroded as the boundary between private and public purposes becomes increasingly fuzzy. Codes may even be viewed as an embodiment of the "anti-Americanism" so prevalent in international organizations.

While it is possible to state such extreme positions, the real world is more complicated. The positions taken with respect to each of the three proposed codes discussed in this study depend on the balancing of factors of a more complex economic, diplomatic, and political nature. These factors must include the impact on U.S. national interests; the achievement of our foreign policy objectives; the impact of code provisions on other countries, especially those of the developing third world; and the objective need for international regulation reflecting U.S. experience and laws. It is against these more particular criteria that each of the three pending codes must be evaluated.

Code of Conduct for Liner Conferences

The Liner Code is quite different from previous international agreements in the shipping field. First, if it comes into force, it would become part of maritime law dealing with commercial affairs. Second, the Liner Code would affect the position of all shipping lines in a trade, even lines of nonsignatories. Shipping lines of countries that do not sign would be "granted" a right to compete for only a small percentage of all cargo and would be subject to the rate and other provisions of the Liner Code as they affect the trade between two signatory nations. This regime would be substantially different from the traditional concept of freedom of the seas in which ships of all countries compete for cargo. Thus the new regime could give rise to numerous disputes.

A number of options are available to the United States in dealing with the code:

- If U.S. policy is essentially neutral, and if the Liner Code comes into force, then U.S. shipping companies would be left to cope with particular problems of dealing with the Liner Code as they occur. U.S. companies may have to withdraw from certain conferences; where they remain, they will find themselves in disputes stemming from conflicts of law. Lastly, shipping companies may seek to escalate specific issues and cases to the governmental level, which could exacerbate relations between the United States and some countries.
- It would be possible to bring U.S. policy into line with the Liner Code by adopting its provisions, thus superseding inconsistent provisions of the Shipping Act. Because the code permits and sanctions certain anticompetitive commercial activities now prohibited, such as cargo sharing and pooling, a fundamental policy reappraisal would be required.
- The United States has made and could continue to make efforts to persuade other governments (at other ends of important U.S. trade routes) that the Liner Code is not beneficial and they should not adopt the Liner Code either as a convention or as domestic law. In fact, the United States, through the OECD and UNCTAD as well as through bilateral contacts, has emphasized the need for trade liberalization rather than trade restriction as embodied in the Liner Code.

Some additional options are available to the United States, given the rather specialized nature of the subject matter. The Federal Maritime Commission could be directed to resolve conflicts between U.S. laws and the Liner Code as they arise. U.S. laws with respect to shipping conferences, cargo sharing, and similar issues could be reexamined in the light of the Liner Code without the United States formally becoming party to the code. Finally, the United States could take the position that, as a matter of law, the Liner Code does not supersede intergovernmental agreements, and the United States could negotiate appropriate intergovernmental agreements (either bilateral or multilateral) on procedures or standards for handling disputes that might arise between the United States and code signatories.[1]

In spite of its specialized nature, the Liner Code is an important indicator of the aspirations and power of developing countries. The Liner Code represents an important exercise of LDC political voting

---

[1] Capone, "Code of Conduct for Liner Conferences," p. 275.

strength, carefully nurtured and orchestrated over a period of several years in the United Nations and UNCTAD. It represents a clearly divisive issue for the developed countries, exposing internal differences within the Western industrialized countries. Further, the code reflects current political attitudes of Western countries. For example, Australia under a Labour government was anxious to show sympathy with the developing world and supported the Liner Code. Australia under a Conservative government and with domestic shipping interests outweighing foreign policy interests found support for the Liner Code waning. Finally, the Liner Code provides a prototype for other codes of conduct now being negotiated. It represents the less developed countries' first solid victory in UNCTAD and therefore lays the groundwork for further UNCTAD efforts in restrictive business practices, commodities, technology transfer, and other commercial areas of interest to the developing countries. It is the first multilateral, potentially universal, intergovernmental code of conduct. It transcends regional codes and partial solutions by attempting to deal on a worldwide basis with a worldwide industry. It is intended to be a binding agreement whose terms would apply to all states adhering to it. And it provides for an international conciliation procedure, a step toward the establishment of an international dispute settlement mechanism in this field.

Code of Conduct on the Transfer of Technology

The Technology Code negotiators faced important issues of concern to both developing and developed countries. The developing countries have obviously, not without some struggle, established the political connection between technology and development. They are interested in pursuing the latter by controlling and using the former. At the other end of the technological transfer process, however, private multinational corporations predominate. Transfers of technology from corporations to developing countries account for only 10 percent of the world's "technology purchases." Is it therefore likely that the developed countries will agree to alter the terms, the conditions, and the international system through which 90 percent of the transfers occur in order to satisfy the needs expressed by the recipients of the other 10 percent? Unless the developing countries can respond to this problem in a satisfactory way, the developed countries will have every right to continue to object to conditions being imposed on them.

The U.S. Department of Justice feels that many of the restrictive business practices provisions proposed by the LDCs for the Technology Code can in fact be acceptably compromised and that a common denominator code can be agreed upon.[2] In that case the United States may even have an interest in seeing a Technology Code in force as a binding legal document. For that decision to be taken, the Technology Code would have to remove or weaken not only many of the objectionable proposals of the Group of Seventy-Seven, but also much of the polemical language against the West, multinational corporations, and technology transferors. We should not accept, for example, misleading and impractical language referring to technology as "the common heritage of mankind" and reminiscent of the Law of the Sea negotiations.

If, on the other hand, the position taken by the Group of Seventy-Seven is inflexible, then the Technology Code will be unacceptable to the technology exporting countries. A text could nevertheless be passed as a resolution by the Group of Seventy-Seven and opened for signature. In this case the convention would, if ratified by a sufficient number of nations, become law in those countries, but presumably no major technology exporters would be among them.

In any case, a Technology Code in itself will not increase the flow of technology. There are no provisions in the Technology Code to improve the environment of the less developed countries to receive technology. There are no incentives to encourage multinational firms to seek opportunities to transfer technology. The regulatory provisions requiring review and registration of contracts will certainly not provide such incentives. Although in some cases there may be an increase in the predictability of government actions, in others there will be an increase in uncertainty. These uncertainties will stem from the interaction of the Technology Code with the national laws of the countries adopting it, the normal uncertainties of administrative and judicial interpretation of any new international instrument, and the insufficiently understood meaning and intent of its provisions. Furthermore, time will be required for the dust to settle and for businessmen to know how to react to the Technology Code, just as they have had to do with respect to the national technology transfer laws and the Andean Code.

Although the U.S. government has recognized the need for technology transfer to developing countries, few government initiatives have been proposed to accomplish it. At the fourth UNCTAD session in Nairobi in 1976, for example, Secretary of State Kissinger gave full but general support to technology transfer initiatives without identify-

---

[2] Joel Davidow of the Antitrust Division of the U.S. Department of Justice at ABA Conference on Restrictive Business Practices and International Transfer of Technology, New York, December 14, 1977.

ing proposals in detail. He did not endorse a legally binding code of conduct, yet it could be fairly argued that he supported the concept.

Within the United States, differences of opinion certainly exist as to the need for a Technology Code. At one extreme are the critics of multinational corporations—development economists and others—who are concerned with the abuses of international businesses, particularly in their dealings with smaller, less powerful countries. At the other extreme are the representatives of the multinational corporations and the patent bar. In the middle may be found some government officials who, while recognizing the private interests involved, nevertheless are seeking ways to work with the developing countries, to assist in their development, and to eliminate restrictive and anticompetitive business practices.

The question therefore remains how important the Technology Code is to the Group of Seventy-Seven and the UN system. If the Technology Code continues to be a major objective of the United Nations as a way of solving development problems, then the secretariat itself may influence the Group of Seventy-Seven to compromise. On the other hand, if the Group of Seventy-Seven cannot find the necessary flexibility and instead votes in a Technology Code over the objections of the technology exporters, then the effort would probably prove to be a failure. The lines would be sharply drawn between the standards of the Technology Code and the actual practices of individual countries. This could eventually lead to more investment disputes, boycotts, expropriations, and tension between the rich and poor nations. Furthermore, the international community, as symbolized by UNCTAD and the United Nations, would have received a major setback in its efforts to regulate international economic affairs. Most important, however, an opportunity to provide real incentives for technology transfer would have been lost.

Code of Conduct for Transnational Corporations

In preparation for the UN Transnational Code negotiations, the U.S. government has already publicly stated its position. The United States believes that multinational corporations have made and should be encouraged to continue to make major contributions to world economic development. The United States nevertheless recognizes the concerns regarding multinational corporations, and supports both the recent OECD Code and constructive international action on investment issues. Codes can be helpful in improving the climate for investment. More specifically, in the President's International Economic Report of 1975 which addressed the Transnational Code, the United

States emphasized that any code dealing with multinational corporations should

- articulate general principles of good business practice applicable to national as well as multinational enterprises and state-owned as well as privately owned enterprises
- be voluntary rather than mandatory
- be nondiscriminatory toward foreign investment
- acknowledge existing principles of international law (especially those governing the treatment of foreigners and their property)
- endorse international arbitration for settling investment disputes
- acknowledge the responsibilities of governments to resolve problems arising from conflicting government requirements
- affirm that governments and enterprises must respect contractual obligations.

The most important development in a related field has been U.S. support for the Common Fund, a mechanism to set the international levels of commodity prices. This suggests that the United States is going to seek ways to reduce tensions with the developing world by supporting initiatives of developing countries that would deal with private concerns through international agreements. It suggests, too, a willingness to override market forces and to support institutional solutions to economic problems. All of these tendencies will work in the direction of U.S. support for the Code of Conduct for Transnational Corporations.

A Transnational Code with broad and sweeping language such as that contained in the annotated outline discussed in chapter 7 could not be enforced. This defect could not be cured by merely increasing specificity since there is insufficient consensus at this point on major objectives and intentions to allow the adoption of enforceable rules.[3] A better approach might be to concentrate action on areas where agreement could be reached; transfer pricing or restrictive business practices are two candidates. Furthermore, disagreement about specific substantive provisions would force compromises in the drafting that could reduce the impact of provisions such as those dealing with enforcement, the expropriation of property, or criminal or civil penalties imposed on corporations or their officers.

---

[3] In fact, one observer concludes "that it is very unlikely that a broad, inclusive and legally enforceable international convention with supranational, adjudicatory and enforcement mechanisms will be adopted in the foreseeable future." Mark R. Joelson and Joseph P. Griffin, "International Regulation of Restrictive Business Practices Engaged in by Transnational Enterprises: A Prognosis," *International Lawyer*, vol. 11, no. 1 (1977), p. 25.

The UN deliberations will also have to deal with the question of the legal nature of a Transnational Code, and whether a violation of it would incur penalties. Developing countries have generally supported this concept, while developed countries, including the United States, have opposed it. The position of the United States may have to be modified. Because the United States has pushed for a mandatory code on illegal payments and bribery, its position of insisting on a voluntary Transnational Code would seem anomalous.[4] Furthermore, a mandatory code may benefit the United States by raising antitrust and competitive standards throughout the world.

As long as the language of the code is general, some developed countries may see it in their political interest to agree to a binding Transnational Code. In their view such a code states broad moral standards that will not and cannot be applied in practice. For this reason, their agreement to the Transnational Code would merely be a political gesture to the LDCs.

Other developed countries may take a much harder line, viewing this Transnational Code as the first step toward development of specific provisions with operative effect. A general code could spawn subsidiary agreements in specific issue areas. One could find support for this concern in the report of the Group of Eminent Persons, which saw the Commission on Transnationals as a forum for discussion and evolution of specific recommendations. The United Nations does not now have codes or resolutions with such operative effect. The Transnational Code could signal a major change.

As an alternative to a single, binding, and all-inclusive Transnational Code, Joelson and Griffin suggest three more modest international conventions.[5] The first would be a convention for international consultation and conciliation, along the lines of GATT. This has been supported by the OECD and UNCTAD's Expert Group on Restrictive Business Practices. The second possibility is the development of model laws for developing countries. Some progress has been made within UNCTAD to formulate model laws on restrictive business practices. Because these model laws are intended to be incorporated in national laws, they do not require either international agreement, supranational regulatory authority, or all-inclusive solutions. Enactment of model laws could achieve some harmonization and may reduce international conflicts. Finally, it might be possible to draft a convention limited to practices that affect only international trade. Thus the activities of multinational corporations in domestic markets

---

[4] Coonrod, "Code of Conduct for Transnational Corporations," p. 297.
[5] Joelson and Griffin, "International Regulation," pp. 25–28.

or commerce that are beyond the normal reach of international law would remain so. There would be substantial international interest in developing rules for such international transactions, and that project may prove more practicable.

The UN's establishment of the Centre on Transnational Corporations and the Commission on Transnationals, as well as the activities of transnational corporations themselves, have attracted a great deal of attention. But the UN's efforts may be made moot by other developments. Forces are already at work to improve national laws and to encourage needed reform of multinational corporation behavior. The vehement criticism of multinational firms so common only a few years ago is no longer as widespread nor as vocal; some of it has even been replaced by moderate and cautious approval. Nevertheless, the commission is considering principles of a draft code that would significantly and adversely affect foreign trade transactions and new investment. Sufficient uncertainty would exist about treatment of multinationals under such a code that needed investments might not be made. This impact would clearly be counterproductive. It is to be hoped that by the time the commission begins to consider specific language, it will be able to make substantive contributions to both the regulation of multinational corporations and the facilitation of their operations.

Some Tentative Conclusions

For a number of reasons, codes of conduct will be increasingly used in the international community to deal with problems which countries are unable to solve on a national level. First, there is competition for investment and for development, especially among the developing countries, and they will seek standardized rules of behavior in order to minimize the competition and eliminate distortions among them. Second, there is momentum within the international community, particularly within the United Nations, "to do something" about the perceived problems of multinational corporate behavior, regardless of the danger of legislating today for yesterday's problems. Third, many of the less developed countries just do not have the expertise or the political will to develop solutions on their own; they feel more comfortable applying U.N.-developed solutions that have the appearance of universality and authority.

Even if negotiated successfully, however, codes of conduct will not be applied consistently, uniformly, or vigorously. To some degree the political, "polemical" purpose will be solved when the codes are negotiated, voted, and adopted. What actually happens in any given country may follow traditional patterns, regardless of what the codes say. In fact, we may see the development of parallel systems of law, with international codes serving as rhetorical and moral standards, but with national laws and regulations continuing to reflect the realities of money and power.

Evidence in support of this proposition comes from the Andean region. The Andean group of countries may be expected to be as homogeneous a group as can be found on the face of the earth, yet they vary considerably in geography, resources, racial makeup, culture, economy, politics, and development status. Even within this relatively small group, widely divergent views exist. Chile dropped out of the Andean group, in part because of the provisions of the investment code; Colombia, Ecuador, and Bolivia are acting slowly; Peru and Venezuela are applying the investment code vigorously; and there are five different interpretations of its provisions. If one expands the sample not just to a part of Latin America but to all of the countries of the world, it is almost inconceivable that, for example, Peru, Uganda, Kuwait, Singapore, Romania, and India, to say nothing of the developed OECD countries, will have the same interests and would apply a code similarly. Therefore, it is unlikely that codes will reflect more than a "paper" consensus.

But even if codes are adopted and effectively implemented, will the result be all that bad for the United States? Clearly, if U.S. objectives are met in the negotiating process, there will be little problem. If the codes are voluntary and nondiscriminatory toward foreign investment, then the United States will have achieved its major objectives. If the codes acknowledge existing principles of law, especially those governing the treatment of the property of foreigners, this would be an even greater achievement in the fostering of a liberal investment system.

If the effect of the codes is to bring foreign standards of doing business up to U.S. standards, then the result could be beneficial to U.S. interests. Assuming that the most objectionable nationalistic features are negotiated out, laws with respect to restrictive business practices in other countries would only be raised to U.S. levels. U.S. antitrust laws have been developed for sound reasons—the protection of competition and free enterprise. To the extent we wish to see the development of more competitive economies in other countries, we should be prepared to assist those countries in developing the institutional preconditions necessary for them. Similarly, the disclosure required of multinational corporation operations in other countries ought to be similar to that in the United States.

But the real possibility exists that codes could be discriminatory, nationalistic, and mandatory, and could fail to embrace any of the stated U.S. objectives. Will this mean an unacceptable environment for U.S. multinational corporations? In my view, it would lead to increased tensions, intergovernmental disputes, hardening of positions between North and South, and a slowing down of the growth of the international economy.

The proper role for the United States in this process is not to object unthinkingly to all proposals for codes. A better approach is to work constructively within the international negotiating system to influence the codes and thus the laws of other countries in directions that are advantageous to the United States. Because we believe that development involves growth, not merely reallocation of existing resources, this approach will be advantageous to other countries. The creation of new jobs and production through investment in other countries must lead to greater wealth throughout the world. The task is not merely to divide the pie, but to make it larger. If our share is growing absolutely, even though declining proportionately, we can achieve much more than self-satisfaction. We can assist in the construction of a truly meaningful, liberal, and workable new international economic order.

Appendix A

OECD Declaration on International Investment and Multinational Enterprises

DECLARATION
ON INTERNATIONAL INVESTMENT
AND MULTINATIONAL ENTERPRISES

THE GOVERNMENTS OF OECD MEMBER COUNTRIES*
CONSIDERING

that international investment has assumed increased importance in the world economy and has considerably contributed to the development of their countries;

that multinational enterprises play an important role in this investment process;

that co-operation by Member countries can improve the foreign investment climate, encourage the positive contribution which multinational enterprises can make to economic and social progress, and minimise and resolve difficulties which may arise from their various operations;

that, while continuing endeavours within the OECD may lead to further international arrangements and agreements in this field, it seems appropriate at this stage to intensify their co-operation and consultation on issues relating to international investment and multinational enterprises through inter-related instruments each of which deals with a different aspect of the matter and together constitute a framework within which the OECD will consider these issues:

DECLARE:

Guidelines for MNE's

I. that they jointly recommend to multinational enterprises operating in their territories the observance of the Guidelines as set forth in the Annex hereto having regard to the considerations and understandings which introduce the Guidelines and are an integral part of them.

---

* The Turkish Government was not in a position to participate in this Declaration.

National Treatment	II.1	that Member countries should, consistent with their needs to maintain public order, to protect their essential security interests and to fulfil commitments relating to international peace and security, accord to enterprises operating in their territories and owned or controlled directly or indirectly by nationals of another Member country (hereinafter referred to as "Foreign-Controlled Enterprises") treatment under their laws, regulations and administrative practices, consistent with international law and no less favourable than that accorded in like situations to domestic enterprises (hereinafter referred to as "National Treatment").
	2	that Member countries will consider applying "National Treatment" in respect of countries other than Member countries.
	3	that Member countries will endeavour to ensure that their territorial subdivisions apply "National Treatment".
	4	that this Declaration does not deal with the right of Member countries to regulate the entry of foreign investment or the conditions of establishment of foreign enterprises.
International Investment Incentives and Disincentives	III.1	that they recognise the need to strengthen their co-operation in the field of international direct investment.
	2	that they thus recognise the need to give due weight to the interests of Member countries affected by specific laws, regulations and administrative practices in this field (hereinafter called "measures") providing official incentives and disincentives to international direct investment.
	3	that Member countries will endeavour to make such measures as transparent as possible, so that their importance and purpose can be ascertained and that information on them can be readily available.
Consultation Procedures	IV	that they are prepared to consult one another on the above matters in conformity with the Decisions of the Council relating to Inter-Governmental Consultation Procedures on the Guidelines for Multinational Enterprises, on National Treatment and on International Investment Incentives and Disincentives.
Review	V	that they will review the above matters within three years with a view to improving the effectiveness of international economic co-

operation among Member countries on issues relating to international investment and multinational enterprises.

ANNEX

TO THE DECLARATION OF 21ST JUNE, 1976 BY GOVERNMENTS OF OECD MEMBER COUNTRIES ON INTERNATIONAL INVESTMENT AND MULTINATIONAL ENTERPRISES

GUIDELINES FOR MULTINATIONAL ENTERPRISES

1. Multinational enterprises now play an important part in the economies of Member countries and in international economic relations, which is of increasing interest to governments. Through international direct investment, such enterprises can bring substantial benefits to home and host countries by contributing to the efficient utilisation of capital, technology and human resources between countries and can thus fulfill an important role in the promotion of economic and social welfare. But the advances made by multinational enterprises in organising their operations beyond the national framework may lead to abuse of concentrations of economic power and to conflicts with national policy objectives. In addition, the complexity of these multinational enterprises and the difficulty of clearly perceiving their diverse structures, operations and policies sometimes give rise to concern.

2. The common aim of the Member countries is to encourage the positive contributions which multinational enterprises can make to economic and social progress and to minimise and resolve the difficulties to which their various operations may give rise. In view of the transnational structure of such enterprises, this aim will be furthered by co-operation among the OECD countries where the headquarters of most of the multinational enterprises are established and which are the location of a substantial part of their operations. The guidelines set out hereafter are designed to assist in the achievement of this common aim and to contribute to improving the foreign investment climate.

3. Since the operations of multinational enterprises extend throughout the world, including countries that are not Members of the Organisation, international co-operation in this field should extend to all States. Member countries will give their full support to efforts undertaken in co-operation with non-Member countries, and in particular with developing countries, with a view to improving the welfare and living standards of all people both by encouraging the positive contributions which multinational enterprises can make and by minimising and resolving the problems which may arise in connection with their activities.

4. Within the Organisation, the programme of co-operation to attain these ends will be a continuing, pragmatic and balanced one. It comes within the general aims of the Convention on the Organisation for Economic Co-operation and Development (O.E.C.D.) and makes full use of the various

specialised bodies of the Organisation, whose terms of reference already cover many aspects of the role of multinational enterprises, notably in matters of international trade and payments, competition, taxation, manpower, industrial development, science and technology. In these bodies, work is being carried out on the identification of issues, the improvement of relevant qualitative and statistical information and the elaboration of proposals for action designed to strengthen inter-governmental co-operation. In some of these areas procedures already exist through which issues related to the operations of multinational enterprises can be taken up. This work could result in the conclusion of further and complementary agreements and arrangements between governments.

5. The initial phase of the co-operation programme is composed of a Declaration and three Decisions promulgated simultaneously as they are complementary and inter-connected, in respect of guidelines for multinational enterprises, national treatment for foreign-controlled enterprises and international investment incentives and disincentives.

6. The guidelines set out below are recommendations jointly addressed by Member countries to multinational enterprises operating in their territories. These guidelines, which take into account the problems which can arise because of the international structure of these enterprises, lay down standards for the activities of these enterprises in the different Member countries. Observance of the guidelines is voluntary and not legally enforceable. However, they should help to ensure that the operations of these enterprises are in harmony with national policies of the countries where they operate and to strengthen the basis of mutual confidence between enterprises and States.

7. Every State has the right to prescribe the conditions under which multinational enterprises operate within its national jurisdiction, subject to international law and to the international agreements to which it has subscribed. The entities of a multinational enterprise located in various countries are subject to the laws of these countries.

8. A precise legal definition of multinational enterprises is not required for the purposes of the guidelines. These usually comprise companies or other entities whose ownership is private, state or mixed, established in different countries and so linked that one or more of them may be able to exercise a significant influence over the activities of others and, in particular, to share knowledge and resources with the others. The degree of autonomy of each entity in relation to the others varies widely from one multinational enterprise to another, depending on the nature of the links between such entities and the fields of activity concerned. For these reasons, the guidelines are addressed to the various entities within the multinational enterprise (parent companies and/or local entities) according to the actual distribution of responsibilities among them on the understanding that they will co-operate and provide assistance to one another as necessary to facilitate observance of the guidelines. The word "enterprise" as used in these guidelines refers to these various entities in accordance with their responsibilities.

9. The guidelines are not aimed at introducing differences of treatment between multinational and domestic enterprises; wherever relevant they

reflect good practice for all. Accordingly, multinational and domestic enterprises are subject to the same expectations in respect of their conduct wherever the guidelines are relevant to both.

10. The use of appropriate international dispute settlement mechanisms, including arbitration, should be encouraged as a means of facilitating the resolution of problems arising between enterprises and Member countries.

11. Member countries have agreed to establish appropriate review and consultation procedures concerning issues arising in respect of the guidelines. When multinational enterprises are made subject to conflicting requirements by Member countries, the governments concerned will co-operate in good faith with a view to resolving such problems either within the Committee on International Investment and Multinational Enterprises established by the OECD Council on 21st January, 1975 or through other mutually acceptable arrangements.

HAVING REGARD to the foregoing considerations, the Member countries set forth the following guidelines for multinational enterprises with the understanding that Member countries will fulfil their responsibilities to treat enterprises equitably and in accordance with international law and international agreements, as well as contractual obligations to which they have subscribed:

General Policies

Enterprises should

(1) take fully into account established general policy objectives of the Member countries in which they operate;

(2) in particular, give due consideration to those countries' aims and priorities with regard to economic and social progress, including industrial and regional development, the protection of the environment, the creation of employment opportunities, the promotion of innovation and the transfer of technology;

(3) while observing their legal obligations concerning information, supply their entities with supplementary information the latter may need in order to meet requests by the authorities of the countries in which those entities are located for information relevant to the activities of those entities, taking into account legitimate requirements of business confidentiality;

(4) favour close co-operation with the local community and business interests;

(5) allow their component entities freedom to develop their activities and to exploit their competitive advantage in domestic and foreign markets, consistent with the need for specialisation and sound commercial practice;

(6) when filling responsible posts in each country of operation, take due account of individual qualifications without discrimination as to nationality, subject to particular national requirements in this respect;

(7) not render—and they should not be solicited or expected to render —any bribe or other improper benefit, direct or indirect, to any public servant or holder of public office;

(8) unless legally permissible, not make contributions to candidates for public office or to political parties or other political organisations;

(9) abstain from any improper involvement in local political activities.

Disclosure of Information

Enterprises should, having due regard to their nature and relative size in the economic context of their operations and to requirements of business confidentiality and to cost, publish in a form suited to improve public understanding a sufficient body of factual information on the structure, activities and policies of the enterprise as a whole, as a supplement, in so far as is necessary for this purpose, to information to be disclosed under the national law of the individual countries in which they operate. To this end, they should publish within reasonable time limits, on a regular basis, but at least annually, financial statements and other pertinent information relating to the enterprise as a whole, comprising in particular:

(i) the structure of the enterprise, showing the name and location of the parent company, its main affiliates, its percentage ownership, direct and indirect, in these affiliates, including shareholdings between them;

(ii) the geographical areas* where operations are carried out and the principal activities carried on therein by the parent company and the main affiliates;

(iii) the operating results and sales by geographical area and the sales in the major lines of business for the enterprise as a whole;

(iv) significant new capital investment by geographical area and, as far as practicable, by major lines of business for the enterprise as a whole;

(v) a statement of the sources and uses of funds by the enterprise as a whole;

(vi) the average number of employees in each geographical area;

(vii) research and development expenditure for the enterprise as a whole;

(viii) the policies followed in respect of intra-group pricing;

---

* For the purposes of the guideline on disclosure of information the term "geographical area" means groups of countries or individual countries as each enterprise determines it appropriate in its particular circumstances. While no single method of grouping is appropriate for all enterprises, or for all purposes, the factors to be considered by an enterprise would include the significance of operations carried out in individual countries or areas as well as the effects on its competitiveness, geographic proximity, economic affinity, similarities in business environments and the nature, scale and degree of interrelationship of the enterprises' operations in the various countries.

(ix) the accounting policies, including those on consolidation, observed in compiling the published information.

Competition

Enterprises should

while conforming to official competition rules and established policies of the countries in which they operate,

(1) refrain from actions which would adversely affect competition in the relevant market by abusing a dominant position of market power, by means of, for example,

    (a) anti-competitive acquisitions,

    (b) predatory behaviour towards competitors,

    (c) unreasonable refusal to deal,

    (d) anti-competitive abuse of industrial property rights,

    (e) discriminatory (i.e. unreasonably differentiated) pricing and using such pricing transactions between affiliated enterprises as a means of affecting adversely competition outside these enterprises;

(2) allow purchasers, distributors and licensees freedom to resell, export, purchase and develop their operations consistent with law, trade conditions, the need for specialisation and sound commercial practice;

(3) refrain from participating in or otherwise purposely strengthening the restrictive effects of international or domestic cartels or restrictive agreements which adversely affect or eliminate competition and which are not generally or specifically accepted under applicable national or international legislation;

(4) be ready to consult and co-operate, including the provision of information, with competent authorities of countries whose interests are directly affected in regard to competition issues or investigations. Provision of information should be in accordance with safeguards normally applicable in this field.

Financing

Enterprises should, in managing the financial and commercial operations of their activities, and especially their liquid foreign assets and liabilities, take into consideration the established objectives of the countries in which they operate regarding balance of payments and credit policies.

Taxation

Enterprises should

(1) upon request of the taxation authorities of the countries in which they operate, provide, in accordance with the safeguards and rele-

vant procedures of the national laws of these countries, the information necessary to determine correctly the taxes to be assessed in connection with their operations, including relevant information concerning their operations in other countries;

(2) refrain from making use of the particular facilities available to them, such as transfer pricing which does not conform to an arm's length standard, for modifying in ways contrary to national laws the tax base on which members of the group are assessed.

Employment and Industrial Relations

Enterprises should

within the framework of law, regulations and prevailing labour relations and employment practices, in each of the countries in which they operate,

(1) respect the right of their employees to be represented by trade unions and other bona fide organisations of employees, and engage in constructive negotiations, either individually or through employers' associations, with such employee organisations with a view to reaching agreements on employment conditions, which should include provisions for dealing with disputes arising over the interpretation of such agreements, and for ensuring mutually respected rights and responsibilities;

(2) (a) provide such facilities to representatives of the employees as may be necessary to assist in the development of effective collective agreements;

(b) provide to representatives of employees information which is needed for meaningful negotiations on conditions of employment;

(3) provide to representatives of employees where this accords with local law and practice, information which enables them to obtain a true and fair view of the performance of the entity or, where appropriate, the enterprise as a whole;

(4) observe standards of employment and industrial relations not less favourable than those observed by comparable employers in the host country;

(5) in their operations, to the greatest extent practicable, utilise, train and prepare for upgrading members of the local labour force in co-operation with representatives of their employees and, where appropriate, the relevant governmental authorities;

(6) in considering changes in their operations which would have major effects upon the livelihood of their employees, in particular in the case of the closure of an entity involving collective lay-offs or dismissals; provide reasonable notice of such changes to representatives of their employees, and where appropriate to the relevant governmental authorities, and co-operate with the employee representative and appropriate governmental authorities so as to mitigate to the maximum extent practicable adverse effects;

(7) implement their employment policies including hiring, discharge, pay, promotion and training without discrimination unless selectivity in respect of employee characteristics is in furtherance of established governmental policies which specifically promote greater equality of employment opportunity;

(8) in the context of bona fide negotiations* with representatives of employees on conditions of employment or while employees are exercising a right to organise, not threaten to utilise a capacity to transfer the whole or part of an operating unit from the country concerned in order to influence unfairly those negotiations or to hinder the exercise of a right to organise;

(9) enable authorised representatives of their employees to conduct negotiations on collective bargaining or labour management relations issues with representatives of management who are authorised to take decisions on the matters under negotiation.

Science and Technology

Enterprises should

(1) endeavour to ensure that their activities fit satisfactorily into the scientific and technological policies and plans of the countries in which they operate, and contribute to the development of national scientific and technological capacities, including as far as appropriate the establishment and improvement in host countries of their capacity to innovate;

(2) to the fullest extent practicable, adopt in the course of their business activities practices which permit the rapid diffusion of technologies with due regard to the protection of industrial and intellectual property rights;

(3) when granting licenses for the use of industrial property rights or when otherwise transferring technology do so on reasonable terms and conditions.

DECISION OF THE COUNCIL
ON INTER-GOVERNMENTAL CONSULTATION
PROCEDURES ON THE GUIDELINES
FOR MULTINATIONAL ENTERPRISES

The Council,

Having regard to the Convention on the Organisation for Economic Co-operation and Development of 14th December, 1960 and, in particular, to Article 2(d), 3 and 5(a) thereof;

---

* Bona fide negotiations may include labour disputes as part of the process of negotiation. Whether or not labour disputes are so included will be determined by the law and prevailing employment practices of particular countries.

Having regard to the Resolution of the Council of 21st January, 1975 establishing a Committee on International Investment and Multinational Enterprises and, in particular, to paragraph 2 thereof [C(74)247 (Final)];

Taking note of the Declaration by the Governments of OECD Member countries of 21st June, 1976 in which they jointly recommend to multinational enterprises the observance of guidelines for multinational enterprises;

Recognising the desirability of setting forth procedures by which consultations may take place on matters related to these guidelines;

On the proposal of the Committee on International Investment and Multinational Enterprises;

DECIDES:

1. The Committee on International Investment and Multinational Enterprises (hereinafter called the "Committee") shall periodically or at the request of a Member country hold an exchange of views on matters related to the guidelines and the experience gained in their application. The Committee shall periodically report to the Council on these matters.

2. The Committee shall periodically invite the Business and Industry Advisory Committee to OECD (BIAC) and the Trade Union Advisory Committee to OECD (TUAC) to express their views on matters related to the guidelines and shall take account of such views in its reports to the Council.

3. On the proposal of a Member country the Committee may decide whether individual enterprises should be given the opportunity, if they so wish, to express their views concerning the application of the guidelines. The Committee shall not reach conclusions on the conduct of individual enterprises.

NOTE: Turkey abstained.

4. Member countries may request that consultations be held in the Committee on any problem arising from the fact that multinational enterprises are made subject to conflicting requirements. Governments concerned will co-operate in good faith with a view to resolving such problems, either within the Committee or through other mutually acceptable arrangements.

5. This Decision shall be reviewed within a period of three years. The Committee shall make proposals for this purpose as appropriate.

DECISION OF THE COUNCIL
ON NATIONAL TREATMENT

The Council,

Having regard to the Convention on the Organisation for Economic Co-operation and Development of 14th December, 1960 and, in particular, Articles 2(c), 2(d), 3 and 5(a) thereof;

Having regard to the Resolution of the Council of 21st January, 1975 establishing a Committee on International Investment and Multinational Enterprises and, in particular, paragraph 2 thereof [C(74)247 (Final)];

Taking note of the Declaration by the Governments of OECD Member countries of 21st June, 1976 on national treatment;

Considering that it is appropriate to establish within the Organisation suitable procedures for reviewing laws, regulations and administrative practices (hereinafter referred to as "measures") which depart from "National Treatment";

On the proposal of the Committee on International Investment and Multinational Enterprises;

DECIDES:

1. Measures taken by a Member country constituting exceptions to "National Treatment" (including measures restricting new investment by "Foreign-Controlled Enterprises" already established in their territory) which are in effect on the date of this Decision shall be notified to the Organisation within 60 days after the date of this Decision.

2. Measures taken by a Member country constituting new exceptions to "National Treatment" (including measures restricting new investment by "Foreign-Controlled Enterprises" already established in their territory taken after the date of this Decision shall be notified to the Organisation within 30 days of their introduction together with the specific reasons therefore and the proposed duration thereof.

3. Measures introduced by a territorial subdivision of a Member country, pursuant to its independent powers, which constitute exceptions to "National Treatment", shall be notified to the Organisation by the Member country concerned, insofar as it has knowledge thereof, within 30 days of the responsible officials of the Member country obtaining such knowledge.

NOTE: Turkey abstained.

4. The Committee on International Investment and Multinational Enterprises (hereinafter called the "Committee") shall periodically review the application of "National Treatment" (including exceptions thereto) with a view to extending such application of "National Treatment." The Committee shall make proposals as and when necessary in this connection.

5. The Committee shall act as a forum for consultations, at the request of a Member country, in respect of any matter related to this instrument and its implementation, including exceptions to "National Treatment" and their application.

6. Member countries shall provide to the Committee, upon its request, all relevant information concerning measures pertaining to the application of "National Treatment" and exceptions thereto.

7. This Decision shall be reviewed within a period of three years. The Committee shall make proposals for this purpose as appropriate.

Decision of the Council
on International Investment Incentives
and Disincentives

The Council,

Having regard to the Convention on the Organisation for Economic Co-operation and Development of 14th December, 1960 and, in particular, Articles 2(c), 2(d), 2(e), 3 and 5(a) thereof;

Having regard to the Resolution of the Council of 21st January, 1975 establishing a Committee on International Investment and Multinational Enterprises and, in particular, paragraph 2 thereof [C(74)247 (Final)];

Taking note of the Declaration by the Governments of OECD Member countries of 21st June, 1976 on international investment incentives and disincentives;

On the proposal of the Committee on International Investment and Multinational Enterprises;

DECIDES:

1. Consultations will take place in the framework of the Committee on International Investment and Multinational Enterprises at the request of a Member country which considers that its interests may be adversely affected by the impact on its flow of international direct investments of measures taken by another Member country specifically designed to provide incentives or disincentives for international direct investment. Having full regard to the national economic objectives of the measures and without prejudice to policies designed to redress regional imbalances, the purpose of the consultations will be to examine the possibility of reducing such effects to a minimum.

2. Member countries shall supply, under the consultation procedures, all permissible information relating to any measures being the subject of the consultation.

3. This Decision shall be reviewed within a period of three years. The Committee on International Investment and Multinational Enterprises shall make proposals for this purpose as appropriate.

NOTE: Turkey abstained.

Appendix B

Draft Codes of Conduct on the Transfer of Technology Proposed by the Group of Seventy-Seven and Group B

ANNEX II

REVISED TEXT OF DRAFT OUTLINE
OF AN INTERNATIONAL CODE OF CONDUCT
ON TRANSFER OF TECHNOLOGY[a]

Contents

Chapter

Note: Parallel lines in the margin indicate formulations which were taken into account in preparing the tentative composite text in annex I above.

---

[a] This text reproduces the draft submitted on behalf of the experts from the Group of Seventy-Seven, as reproduced in TD/AC.1/7, annex II, incorporating the revisions and amendments submitted on behalf of the Group of Seventy-Seven at the third session of the Intergovernmental Group.

[b] Text revised at the third session of the Intergovernmental Group of Experts and circulated (TD/AC.1/WG.1/CRP.7) in Working Group I at the session.

[c] This text was amended informally during the second session in Working Group II.

Preamble

The Contracting Parties,

1. *Recognizing* the paramount role of science and technology for socio-economic development of all countries, and in particular, in the acceleration of the development of the developing countries;

2. *Believing* that technology is a part of universal human heritage and that all countries have the right of access to technology, in order to improve the standards of living of their peoples;

3. *Bearing in mind* relevant decisions and resolutions of the General Assembly and other bodies of the United Nations, in particular UNCTAD, on the transfer and development of technology;

4. *Recognizing* the need to facilitate and encourage the growth of the scientific and technological capabilities of all countries, particularly the developing countries, so that an adequate transfer and development of technology will become an effective instrument for the establishment of a New International Economic Order;

5. *Recognizing* further the need to grant special treatment to the developing countries in their technology transfer transactions;

6. *Drawing attention* to the need of having an unrestricted flow of technological information and in particular to facilitate the flood of information on the availability of alternative technologies and for the selection of appropriate technologies suited to the specific needs of the developing countries;

7. *Affirming* that the Code of Conduct for the transfer of technology shall be universally applicable and therefore all countries should ensure that their enterprises, whether private or public, shall conform in all respects to the provisions of this Code;

8. *Convinced* that an international legally binding instrument is the only form capable of effectively regulating the transfer of technology;

Agree on the adoption of this international legally binding Code of Conduct on transfer of technology.

Chapter I. Principles and Objectives

1.1. The Code of Conduct is based, *inter alia*, on the following principles and objectives

(i) Facilitating and increasing the international flow of proprietary and non-proprietary technology under fair and reasonable terms and conditions to all countries particularly to and from the developing countries;

(ii) Increasing the contributions of technology to the identification and solution of specific problems of all countries, particularly the special problems of developing countries;

(iii) Strengthening the national capabilities of all countries, in particular of developing countries, for selecting imported technologies, assimilating them into their national economies and adapting them creatively to domestic conditions, as well as for the development of indigenous technology and for ensuring the increasing participation of these countries in world production and exchange of technology;

(iv) To establish general equitable rules for the international transfer of technology, taking into consideration particularly the needs of developing countries and the legitimate interests of technology suppliers and technology recipients;

(v) To improve access to technology especially for developing countries, at fair and reasonable prices and costs, both direct and indirect, and to regulate business practices, particularly those arising from transfer pricing and transfer accounting;

(vi) To eliminate restrictive practices arising out of or affecting technology transactions;

(vii) To promote unpackaging of transactions involving transfer of technology with regard to the choice of various elements of technology, evaluation of costs, organizational forms and institutional channels for the transfer;

(viii) To establish an appropriate set of guarantees to suppliers and recipients of technology, taking fully into account the weaker position of recipient enterprises in developing countries; and

(ix) To facilitate an orderly implementation of national laws and policies on transfer of technology through the establishment of minimum international standards.

Chapter II. Definitions and Scope of Application

A. *Definitions*

2.1. For the purposes of this code:

(a) the term "party" means any person, both natural and juridical, of public or private law, either individual or collective, including corporations, companies, partnerships and other associations and organizations, whether owned, controlled or created by individuals, juridical persons, governments, society or any combination thereof, when it engages in international transfer of technology. The term includes branches, subsidiaries and affiliates of foreign corporations and enterprises with varying degrees of foreign ownership. The term also applies to States and international organizations when they engage in international transfer of technology.

(b) the term "acquiring party" means the party which obtains a license, purchases or otherwise acquires technology.

(c) the term "supplying party" means the party which licenses, sells, assigns or otherwise provides technology.

(d) the term "technology receiving country" means the country where the technology provided by the supplying party is to be put to use.

B. *Scope of Application*

2.2 This Code shall apply to any transactions, agreements or arrangements between parties, irrespective of their legal form, which have as their purpose or as one of their purposes the licensing or assignment of industrial property rights, the sale or any other type of transfer of technical knowledge, and the supply of technical services. It shall apply to the transfer of production, management or marketing technologies by any means, excluding the mere sale of goods. Further, the Code shall apply to such international transactions, agreements or arrangements as are entered into between parties which do not reside or are not established in the same country, as well as to transactions, agreements or arrangements between parties which are residents of or established in the same country when at least one party is a branch, subsidiary, affiliate or is otherwise controlled by a foreign entity or when it acts as an intermediary in the transfer of foreign owned technology.

2.3 The Code shall apply, *inter alia*, to the following international transactions, agreements or arrangements for the transfer of technology:

(i) Assignment, sale and licensing transactions covering all forms of industrial property including patents, inventors certificates, utility models, industrial designs, trade marks, service names, and trade names;

(ii) Arrangements covering the provision of know-how and technical expertise in the form of feasibility studies, plans, diagrams, models, instructions, guides, formulae, the supply of services, specifications and/or involving technical, advisory and managerial personnel, and personnel training as well as equipment for training;

(iii) Arrangements covering the provision of basic or detailed engineering designs, the installation and operation of plant and equipment;

(iv) Purchases, leases and other forms of acquisition of machinery, equipment, intermediate goods and/or raw materials, in so far as they are part of transactions, arrangements or agreements involving technology transfers;

(v) Industrial and technical co-operation arrangements of any kind including turn-key agreements, international sub-contracting as well as provision of management and marketing services.

2.4. The provisions of the Code of Conduct shall be universally applicable to all countries and to all transactions, agreements or arrangements, which involve, implicitly or explicitly, an international transfer of technology, regardless of (a) the parties involved, whether private, public, social, regional, sub-regional or international; (b) the levels of development of the countries concerned; and (c) the type of economic, social or political system of the countries among which technology is transferred.

Chapter III. National Regulation of Transfer of Technology Transactions

3.1. In exercising their right to adopt legislation, policies and/or rules for the regulation of transfer of technology operations, States may adopt such measures as evaluation, negotiation, registration and renegotiation of agreements and arrangements involving technology transactions.

3.2. In this connexion each State may, *inter alia*, adopt the following measures:

(i) Regulation of terms and conditions of agreements and arrangements governing transfer of technology;

(ii) Regulation for the prevention of ultimate loss of ownership and/or control of domestic recipient enterprises to foreign interests as a condition to or as a result of the transfer of technology;

(iii) Stipulation that foreign collaboration arrangements must not displace national enterprises from the domestic market;

(iv) Choice of channels, mechanisms and organizational forms for the transfer of technology;

(v) Regulation of the level of domestic credit facilities that may be made available to foreign owned or controlled enterprises involved in the transfer of technology, as well as requirement for adequate assurances of related foreign financing where it forms part of the transfer of technology arrangement;

(vi) Requirement of specifying distinctly as far as may be deemed necessary, each item in a technology package for which payments have to be made by the recipient, and the duration and other modalities of such payments;

(vii) Regulation of the level and modalities of payments and remittances related to the transfer of technology operations, including foreign exchange obligations, prices for imported inputs and the tax treatment to be accorded to such transactions.

(viii) Treatment of payments for technology as profits where there exist relations between or among subsidiaries and parent companies, and also where the supplier and the recipient enterprises form an economic unit or have community of interest, as well as when the effective technical, administrative, financial or commercial management is not exercised by local residents of the recipient country;

(ix) Assist interested parties in the evaluation, negotiation and renegotiation of technology transactions in accordance with the socio-economic conditions and needs, priorities, and laws, regulations, rules and policies of the recipient country;

(x) Define the scope and objective of the transactions, the rights and mitigations of the parties, the price and levels and modalities of payments, the relation and other relevant elements of the arrangements for the screening and registration of technology transactions;

(xi) Establish or strengthen mechanisms in administrative systems for proper enforcement of the rights and obligations flowing from the technology transfer transactions.

Chapter IV. The Regulation of Practices and Arrangements Involving the Transfer of Technology

4.1. Transfer of technology transactions shall not include practices or arrangements which impose restrictions that directly or indirectly have or may have adverse effects on the national economy of the receiving country and/or impose restrictions or limitations on the development of technological capabilities of the receiving country.

4.2.* Parties to transfer of technology transactions shall not make use, *inter alia*, of the following practices and arrangements, whether written or not:

(a) Those practices and arrangements concerning the use, adaptation and assimilation of technology and development of technological capabilities of the technology receiving country:

> (1/2) Restrictions, prohibitions or obligations of any type on exploitation of technology after the normal expiration, invalidation or termination of the transfer of technology transaction, or after the expiration or invalidation of the industrial property rights involved.

> (3) Restricting the field of use of the subject matter of the patented technology.

> (4) Requiring directly or indirectly the acquiring party to transfer or grant back unilaterally to the supplying party improvements arising from the acquired technology, on an exclusive basis or without reciprocal obligations from the supplying party.

> (5)[a] Limitations upon the diffusion and/or further use of technology already imported.

> (6) Obligation upon the recipient to introduce unnecessary design changes and new material specifications imposed by the technology supplier;

> (7) Restriction upon the recipient from adapting the imported technology to local conditions and innovating on the supplied technology;

> (8) Limitations on the research and development policy and activities on the recipient enterprise.

(b) Those practices and arrangements concerning further acquisition of technology by the acquiring party:

> (9) Restrictions on obtaining competing or complementary technology through patents and know-how from other sources with regard to the sale or manufacture of competing products;

> (10) Restrictions on obtaining competing or complementary technology from other supplier with regard to the sale

---

* For purposes of comparison, the numbering used in this revised section follows, as appropriate, the numbering of the earlier draft of chapter IV as reproduced in TD/AC.1/4, annex I, and as reproduced in TD/AC.1/7, annex II.

[a] The former subparagraph (5) of the earlier draft of chapter IV, as reproduced in TD/AC.1/7, annex II, is partially replaced by the new subparagraph (5), as reproduced *supra* and partially replaced by the new subparagraph (31), as reproduced *infra*.

or manufacture of products involving trade marks or trade names;

(11) Restrictions on the freedom of the acquiring party to enter into sales or representation agreements related to similar or competing technologies or products;

(12) Limitation upon the access of the recipient to new technological developments and improvements related to the technology supplied.

(c) Those practices and arrangements concerning the commercial and technological freedom of the acquiring party:

(13) Restrictions on the recipient's volume, scope and/or range of production and/or field of activity;

(14/15)[b] (i) Restrictions by the supplying party regarding the sources of supply of inputs, spare parts, equipment and other products including those bearing a particular trade mark or regarding the sources of technical and managerial personnel.

(ii) Requiring acceptance of additional technology, goods or services not needed or not wanted by the acquiring party or the technology receiving country as a condition for obtaining the technology required.

(16) Obligation upon the recipient to purchase future invention and improvements in the technology from the original supplier;

(17) Use of quality controls or standards by the supplier as means of imposing unwarranted obligations on the technology recipients;

(18) [Replaced by (14/15) above.]

(19) Requirements to use personnel designated by the technology suppliers, beyond the period sufficient for the training of the recipient's personnel, or limitations in the use of personnel of recipient country;

(20) Reservation of the right by the supplier to fix the sale or resale price of the products manufactured;

(21) Requiring the acquiring party to give exclusive sales or representation rights to the supplying party, with due regard to sub-contracting arrangements;

(22)[c] Restrictions on exports resulting directly or indirectly from the technology supplied, including trade mark ar-

---

[b] These provisions also replace subparagraphs (18) and (28) of the earlier draft of chapter IV, as reproduced in TD/AC.1/4, annex I.

[c] This revised provision also replaces subparagraph (27) of the earlier draft of chapter IV, as reproduced in TD/AC.1/4, annex I.

rangements, in the form of restrictions to certain markets, permission to export only to certain markets, and requirements of prior approval of the supplying party for exports and prices of products;

(23) Obligations to use a particular trade mark or trade name or to mention the supplier's name together with the technology acquired;

(24) The use of the privilege granted under the trade mark system to restrict unduly the recipient's activities;

(25) Regulations which restrict or subject to approval by the supplier, the publicity or advertisement to be carried out by the recipient;

(26) Requirements by the supplier, except in management contracts, to participate in the management decisions of the recipient enterprise;

(27) [Replaced by (22) above.]

(28) [Replaced by (14/15) above.]

(d) Those practices and arrangements concerning payments for the transfer of technology:

(29) Obliging the recipient to convert technology payments into capital stock;

(30) Continuation of payments for unused or unexploited technology;

(31)[d] Requiring excessive or double payments by the acquiring party for technology supplied, as by additional payments for the repeated use of the same technology, or by charging fixed minimum payments irrespective of production performance, or by increasing payments progressively with increased output or sales, or by higher rates for output or sales for export vis-à-vis domestic output or sales, or by charging in a cumulative manner on the component parts in addition to the final product as a whole so that total payments are larger than if the same payment were applied on a net-value-added basis.

(32) [Replaced by (31) above.]

(33) Requiring payment on the patents and other industrial property rights not registered in the recipient's country;

(34) Requiring payments by the recipient enterprise for technology imported by the enterprise under earlier arrangements or already available in the country;

(35) [Replaced by (31) above.]

---

[d] This revised provision also replaces subparagraphs (32) and (35) of the earlier draft of chapter IV, as reproduced in TD/AC.1/7, annex II and replaced part of subparagraph (5) of the earlier draft of chapter IV, as reproduced in TD/AC.1/7, annex II.

(e) Those practices and arrangements concerning the duration of the transaction:

(36)[e] Unlimited or unduly long duration of transfer of technology arrangements.

(37) [Replaced by (36) above.]

(38) Requiring the acquiring party in any form to refrain, directly or indirectly, from challenging the validity of patents or other industrial property rights involved in the transfer or the validity of other patents or industrial property rights claimed or obtained by the supplying party.

(39) Practices and arrangements that exempt the supplier from any liability consequent upon defects in the goods produced by the recipient with the help of the technology acquired;

(40) Any practice or arrangement not specifically set forth in (1) through (39) of this section that has an adverse effect on the recipient and that is imposed as a condition for obtaining the technology required;

4.3. Transfer of technology transactions or practices described in section 4.2. are incompatible with the principles and objectives of the Code and shall be null and void.

4.4. Notwithstanding section 4.3. of this chapter, transfer of technology transactions or practices and arrangements contained therein shall be deemed valid if, based upon exceptional circumstances, it is determined by the competent national authority of the technology receiving country that it is in its public interest and that on balance the effect on its national economy will not be adverse.

4.5. Cartel and other collusive activities, whether international or national, among technology suppliers, including those between and among parent companies, their subsidiaries, and their affiliates, which involve restrictions on prices, quantities, territories, customers, as well as market allocation, that have adverse effects on the transfer of technology, shall be utilized. These include, *inter alia*, the following:

(i) Import cartels;

(ii) Export cartels;

(iii) Rebate cartels and other price fixing arrangements;

(iv) International cartels which allocate markets;

(v) Private and semi-official agreements on certain standards in technology supplying countries; and

(vi) Specialization and rationalization cartels leading to a dominant position.

---

[e] This provision also replaces subparagraph (37) of the earlier draft of chapter IV, as reproduced in TD/AC.1/7, annex II.

Chapter V. Guarantees

5.1. The enterprises supplying technology shall guarantee that:

(i) The technology acquired is suitable for the manufacture of products covered by the arrangement;

(ii) The content of the technology transferred is full and complete for the purposes of the arrangement;

(iii) The technology obtained will be capable of achieving a predetermined level of production under the conditions specified in the agreement;

(iv) National personnel shall be adequately trained for service in the recipient country in the knowledge of the technology to be acquired including operation and management techniques of the enterprises;

(v) The recipient shall have access to all improvements upon the techniques in question during the lifetime of the arrangement;

(vi) Where the recipient of the technology has no other alternative than acquiring capital goods, intermediate inputs and/or raw materials from the technology supplier or any other enterprise designated by him, the prices of the articles shall not be higher than current international price levels;

(vii) Where the recipient of the technology has no other alternative than selling his output to the technology supplier or any other enterprises designated by him, the prices of the articles shall not be lower than current international price levels;

(viii) Spare parts, components and other requirements necessary for using the imported technology shall, if required by the recipient, be provided for a specified period of time and without additional charges for maintaining this guarantee;

(ix) The technology suppliers, while drawing up the design specifications of plants, will take fully into account the possibility of utilizing locally available resources.

5.2. The enterprises receiving technology shall in accordance with the spirit and the standards of the Code, guarantee that:

(i) The technology acquired will be used as specified in the arrangement;

(ii) All legitimate payments as specified in the arrangement shall be made to the technology supplier;

(iii) Technical secrets as defined in the arrangement shall be honoured during the duration of the arrangement;

(iv) The quality standards of the products specified in the contract will be reached and maintained where the contract includes the use of suppliers' trade marks, trade name or similar identification of goodwill.

5.3. Governments of technology-receiving countries may require, *inter alia*, that the following guarantees are included in technology transfer arrangements:

(i) The technology is the most adequate to meet the particular technological requirements of the recipient given the supplier's technological capabilities;

(ii) Local consultancy organizations, technical skills and research and development experience will be fully utilized in the selection of the technology and engineering involved in the use of it;

(iii) The undertaking to explore on a continuous basis the possibility of substituting local inputs for imported materials, equipment and spare parts used in the production process;

(iv) More favourable terms granted by the supplier to a recipient should be extended to subsequent recipients in similar positions within the same country;

(v) The parties make full use of the technology already available or being developed in the recipient country;

(vi) The parties to the transfer of technology arrangement devote adequate resources to research and development activities in the recipient country;

(vii) The achievement, as may be agreed, of a predetermined volume of exports;

(viii) National personnel of the recipient country are involved in all the aspects of the technology transfer arrangement including the feasibility and design studies.

Chapter VI.[a] Special Treatment for Developing Countries and International Collaboration

A. *Special treatment for developing countries*

6.1. Governments of developed countries, in order to co-operate toward initiating and strengthening the scientific and technological capabilities of developing countries, shall take adequate specific measures to accord special treatment to developing countries, to fulfil, *inter alia*, the following goals:

(i) Facilitate access by developing countries to information regarding the availability, characteristics, cost and location of alternative technologies that are useful and required by them for their economic and social development;

(ii) Give developing countries the fullest access to technologies whose transfer is subject to governmental decision;

(iii) Give access to available scientific and industrial research data in order to enable developing countries to assess available technologies, to adapt technology to their needs, and to develop national technologies;

(iv) Co-operate in the development of scientific and technological resources in developing countries, with, in particular, the growth of their innovative capacity;

---

[a] The text of this chapter replaces chapters VI and VII of the earlier draft of the Group of Seventy-Seven, as reproduced in TD/AC.1/4, annex I.

(v) Co-operate in measures leading to greater utilization of the managerial, engineering, design and technical experience of the personnel and the institutions of developing countries in specific development projects undertaken at the bilateral or multilateral levels;

(vi) Establish national, regional and/or international institutions, including technology transfer centres, to help the developing countries to obtain their technological requirements for the establishment, construction and operation of plants under the most favourable terms and conditions;

(vii) Promote technical assistance and regional specialization, research and development, and production activities.

6.2. Governments of developed countries shall take the measures necessary to ensure that their technology supplying enterprises shall extend special treatment to developing countries, with respect to the cost and all other terms and conditions of transfer of technology. Measures to this end shall, *inter alia*, include:

(i) Preferential tax treatment, in the country of the technology supplier, of income arising from technology transfer arrangements to developing countries;

(ii) Establishing preferential measures to ensure that the industrial property rights granted to a patent holder in technology supplying countries should not be used by him to restrict imports or products from developing countries;

(iii) Untying of credits and granting of credits on terms more favourable than the usual commercial terms for financing the acquisition of capital and intermediate goods in connexion with technology transactions;

(iv) Encourage their enterprises and institutions to develop technology appropriate to the needs of the developing countries, disseminate such technology to them on equitable terms and conditions, and undertake in these countries research and development activities of interest to them;

(v) Fiscal and other incentives to the technology exporting enterprises for encouraging the development of technological capabilities in enterprises in developing countries, including special training as required by the recipients;

(vi) Fiscal and other incentives to the technology exporting enterprises in developed countries for increasing the proportion of their R and D activities located in developing countries and encouraging their adaptation to conditions and factor endowments prevailing in developing countries.

6.3. The special treatment to developing countries under this Code shall be extended on a non-discriminatory basis and with particular consideration for the special problems and conditions of the least developed among the developing countries.

B. *International collaboration*

6.4. The States recognize the need for appropriate international collaboration among all Governments, intergovernmental bodies, and organs and agencies of the United Nations system with a view to promoting the principles and objectives of this Code and assuring the effective implementation of its provisions.

6.5. Through bilateral, sub-regional, regional and interregional co-operation arrangements aimed at the implementation of this Code, the States may take *inter alia* the following measures:

(a) Exchange of information relating to:

    (i)   the availability, characteristics, costs and location of technology;

    (ii)   technological alternatives and the terms and conditions of transfer of technology;

    (iii)   development and improvement of legislation on transfer of technology and on industrial property;

    (iv)   trends and developments in the practices related to the international transfer of technology;

    (v)   application and enforcement by national authorities of laws and policies on transfer of technology;

    (vi)   the application and effects of this Code.

(b) Harmonization of national legislation and policies concerning transfer of technology, including particularly registration, screening and monitoring of technology transfer agreements, and the implementation of such laws and policies;

(c) Implementation of legislation and policies, including their institutional aspects, concerning technology transfer transactions;

(d) The establishment of common policies and programmes for searching for, acquiring and disseminating technologies available at the national, regional or international levels;

(e) Establishment of programmes for the adaptation, promotion and development of technology in the context of industrial and development objectives;

(f) Implementation and promotion of technical co-operation and of regional specialization, research and development, and production activities.

6.7. All international organizations, and in particular UNCTAD, within the limits of their competence, should be encouraged to assist their member States in the application and effective implementation of the Code, *inter alia*, through promoting and strengthening national and regional action for the implementation of the Code.

(7.4.)[b] The appropriate organs to be established or designated by the States at the time when this Code will enter into force shall be responsible for reviewing the implementation of its provisions.

---

[b] These sections, which were sections 7.4. and 7.5. of chapter VII of the Group of Seventy-Seven text as reproduced in annex I of TD/AC.1/4, are currently under review with a view to the preparation of a revised text on the subjects dealt within them.

(7.5.)[b] In support of the implementation of this Code, the appropriate organs of UNCTAD shall perform the following functions:

(i) Gathering and disseminating information on technological alternatives and on terms and conditions of transfer of technology arrangements;

(ii) Collecting and disseminating information on laws, regulations and policies pursued at the national, regional and international levels concerning technology transfer arrangements;

(iii) Keeping under continuous review the structure of and current practices regarding technology transfer, with special reference to the developing countries;

(iv) Providing a forum for the discussion of the issues dealt with in this Code and reviewing the reports received from Governments on their implementation of the Code;

(v) Undertaking systematic studies and research on the subject of the implementation of the principles and provisions of this Code and making appropriate recommendations to the States.

---

[b] These sections, which were sections 7.4. and 7.5. of chapter VII of the Group of Seventy-Seven text as reproduced in annex I of TD/AC.1/4, are currently under review with a view to the preparation of a revised text on the subjects dealt within them.

Chapter VII[a]

Chapter VIII. Applicable Law and Settlement of Disputes

8.1. Technology transfer arrangements shall be governed, with regard to their validity, performance and interpretation, by the laws of the technology-receiving country.

8.2. The technology-receiving country shall exercise legal jurisdiction over the settlement of disputes pertaining to transfer of technology arrangements between the parties concerned.

8.3. If the laws applicable to the technology transfer arrangements do not exclude resource to arbitration in this field and the parties concerned agree to submit their possible disputes to arbitration, such disputes will be settled according to the procedures agreed upon by the parties concerned.

Chapter IX. Final Provisions

[To be drafted]

---

[a] See footnote a to chapter VI above.

Outline of a Code of Conduct Consisting
of Guidelines for the International
Transfer of Technology[a]

Contents

Chapter

Note: Parallel lines in the margin indicate formulations which were taken into account in preparing the tentative composite text in annex I above.

Preamble

The Participating Countries

1. *Recognizing* the fundamental role of science and technology in the economic and social development of all countries, and in particular, in the promotion of the development of the developing countries;

2. *Recognizing* the benefits to be derived from a universally acceptable code of conduct on the international transfer of technology setting forth general and equitable principles based on mutual respect for the legitimate interests of all parties to the transfer as well as of governments;

3. *Recalling* that the United Nations General Assembly stressed that all countries should facilitate the access of developing countries to the achievements of science and technology, the transfer of technology and the creation of indigenous technology for the benefit of the developing countries;

4. *Believing* that a code of conduct can create an environment which will assist the developing countries in their selection, acquisition and effective use of technology appropriate to their needs in order to develop improved economic standards and living conditions;

5. *Believing* that a code of conduct can help create conditions conducive to increased trade and investment, thereby promoting the international transfer of technology;

---

[a] This text reproduces the draft submitted on behalf of the experts from Group B as reproduced in TD/AC.1/7, annex III.

Hereby set forth the following code of conduct consisting of guidelines for the international transfer of technology:

Chapter I. Definitions and Scope of Application

1.1 For the purposes of the Code of Conduct:

(a) An "international transfer of technology" occurs when technology of a proprietary or non-proprietary nature and/or rights related thereto is transferred across national boundaries from a Supplying Party to a Recipient Party.

(b) "Party" means a person, either natural or juridical, of public or private law, either individual or collective, and includes corporations, companies, partnerships and other associations and organizations, whether owned, controlled, organized or created by governments, individuals, juridical persons or any combination thereof. The term includes joint ventures, as well as any subsidiaries or affiliates. This term also includes States, government agencies, international, regional and sub-regional organizations when they carry out international transfers of technology for commercial purposes.

(c) "Recipient party" means the party which imports technology in a particular transfer of technology transaction.

(d) "Supplying party" means the party which exports technology in a particular transfer of technology transaction.

1.2. The transfer of technology comprises any or all of the following:

(a) Assignment, sale and licensing agreements covering legally protected inventions.

(b) Arrangements covering the provision of know-how and technical expertise in the form of feasibility studies, plans, diagrams, models, instructions, guides, formulae, service contracts, specifications and/or involving technical advisory and managerial personnel and personnel training as well as equipment for training.

(c) Arrangements covering the provision of basic or detailed engineering designs, the installation, operation and functioning of plant and equipment, and turn-key agreements.

1.3. The transfer of technology extends also to the following if they are an integral part of an agreement or arrangement specified in paragraph 1.2.

(a) Assignment, sale and licensing agreements covering forms of industrial property other than those referred to in paragraph 1.2.(a).

(b) Purchases, leases and other forms of acquisition of machinery, equipment, intermediate goods and/or raw materials.

1.4. The transfer of technology does not extend to transactions involving only the sale of goods.

1.5. The Code of Conduct shall be universal in scope, covering all specified acts or agreements comprising the international transfer of technology on a commercial basis, and addressed to all parties engaged in the international transfer of technology as well as to governments, regardless of (a) the type

116

of economic and political system of the countries among which technology is transferred; and (b) the levels of development of the countries concerned.

Chapter II. Objectives and Principles

2.1. The Code of Conduct for the transfer of technology sets out general and equitable guidelines, universally applicable to the international transfer of technology, taking into account the legitimate interests of all parties to the transfer, as well as those of governments. The Code of Conduct will enable all parties to the transfer to be aware of those factors which would encourage, facilitate and maximize the orderly transfer of appropriate technology under mutually satisfactory terms and conditions. Due recognition is given to the particular needs and problems of developing countries, in order that this Code of Conduct assist the developing countries in their efforts to fulfil their economic and social development objectives.

2.2. The Code of Conduct has the following objectives:

(i) To encourage and facilitate the access to and the international flow of proprietary and non-proprietary technology under fair and reasonable and mutually-agreed terms and conditions.

(ii) To contribute to the establishment of a just and mutually satisfactory basis for negotiations between parties to technology transfer transactions thereby promoting mutual confidence between parties as well as governments.

(iii) To facilitate and encourage the growth of the scientific and technological capabilities of all countries including the ability to develop indigenous technology so that all countries may participate in world production and exchange of technology.

(iv) To facilitate the formulation of national policies and the adoption of appropriate national laws and regulations on the subject of transfer of technology.

(v) To identify an appropriate set of responsibilities for supplying and recipient parties to transfer of technology transactions.

(vi) To avoid those restrictive business practices, as defined in Chapter V below which adversely affect transfer of technology.

(vii) To improve the availability of technological information needed to assist parties in the selection of technologies relevant to their needs.

2.3. The Code of Conduct is based on the following principles:

(i) The Code of Conduct is of a general and voluntary nature and therefore does not derogate from legal obligations, including those of States under customary international law or as set forth in treaties, other international agreements or contracts.

(ii) The separate responsibilities of parties to a transfer of technology transaction on the one hand and governments when not acting as parties on the other should be clearly distinguished.

(iii) The Code of Conduct recognizes the right of each government to employ all appropriate means of facilitating and regulating the transfer of technology, with full and complete freedom of decision, including the right to legislate on the subject, within the framework of international law and with due recognition of existing rights and obligations.

(iv) Each technology transaction is an individual case and the transfer of technology is an on-going and sequential process. Flexibility in the technology transfer process is necessary and the freedom of parties to negotiate, conclude and perform agreements for the transfer of technology on mutually acceptable terms and conditions should not be unduly restricted.

(v) Respect by parties and governments for industrial property protection is necessary, in order to provide incentives for research, invention, development, disclosure and transfer of technology.

(vi) Mutual benefits must accrue to technology suppliers and recipients in order to maintain and increase the international flow of technology.

(vii) The parties to a technology transfer agreement should be free to have recourse to appropriate methods of dispute settlement including international arbitration.

Chapter III. National Regulation of Transfer of Technology Transactions

Source and recipient governments:

3.1. Source and recipient governments have the right to adopt legislation, regulations and policies pertaining to the transfer of technology within the framework of applicable international law, treaties and agreements.

3.2. Laws, regulations and policies (including economic and social development objectives) should be premised upon recognition of the importance of: (a) the transfer, on reasonable and mutually-agreed terms and conditions, of technology to recipient countries for the purpose of assisting these countries to achieve their economic and social development objectives, and (b) the promotion of an economic and legal climate conducive to the flow of technology and permitting technology transfers to benefit to the utmost all parties concerned on an equitable basis.

3.3. Laws, regulations and policies (including economic and social development objectives) pertaining to the transfer of technology should be publicly available and provided, along with other relevant information in the area of technology transfer, to the parties engaged in transfer of technology transactions.

3.4. Laws, regulations and policies (including economic and social development objectives) pertaining to the transfer of technology should be applied predictably and equitably.

3.5. Changes in legislation, regulations and their implementation should be carried out with full regard for the existing rights of source and recipient enterprises where contractual and other legal obligations are involved.

3.6. Source and recipient governments should provide through national legislation and regulation, and accession to relevant international agreements, appropriate systems for the legal protection of industrial property rights and for co-operation in exchanging information and experience in the transfer of these rights and the administration of these systems, thereby facilitating and encouraging the development and transfer of technology.

118

Chapter IV. Responsibilities of Source and Recipient Enterprises

To ensure the maximum mutual benefit of all parties to technology transfer agreements.

4.1. Source enterprises should:

(i) Be responsive, to the extent practicable, to the economic and social development objectives of recipient countries in planning the employment of appropriate technology;

(ii) Agree to reasonable terms and conditions when technology is transferred, including licence fees, royalties and other charges;

(iii) Be responsive to inquiries about the unpackaging of transferred technology by making known the various elements included in a particular technology, it being recognized that there are instances where the success of a technology rests in its application as a whole.

(iv) Co-operate, to the extent practicable and appropriate, in the development of the scientific and technological resources of recipient enterprises, and the creation of innovative capacity, including, wherever practicable, the training of recipient enterprise employees;

(v) Utilize, to the extent practicable, materials, labour and technology available in the recipient country with a view to supporting the recipient country's economic and social development objectives;

(vi) Guarantee that (a) the technology meets the description contained in the technology transfer agreement; (b) the technology, properly used, is suitable for the use specifically set forth in the technology transfer agreement.

4.2. Recipient enterprises should:

(i) When negotiating with potential source enterprises, provide appropriate information regarding relevant economic and social development objectives and legislation of the recipient country, and such other information as may be required so as to apprise potential source enterprises of all conditions and circumstances relevant to the transfer and use of technology, including the recipient enterprises' ability effectively to utilize the technology transferred;

4.3. Source and recipient enterprises should:

(i) Comply with all applicable laws and regulations;

(ii) Respect their agreements related to the transfer of technology;

(iii) Agree to (a) appropriate dispute settlement arrangements such as impartial fact-finding and arbitration procedures, and (b) applicable law to be followed in connexion with such arrangements;

(iv) Observe fair and honest business practices in all aspects of technology transfer transactions;

(v) Preserve the confidentiality and proprietary nature of trade secrets and know-how acquired in connexion with the transfer of technology;

(vi) Preserve the confidentiality of all other secret information acquired in connexion with the transfer of technology;

(vii) Take all steps which could reasonably be expected in order to enable themselves to carry out their obligations under a technology transfer agreement including the obligation of recipient enterprises to effect full payment of the agreed price.

Chapter V. Restrictive Business Practices

5.1. Taking into account the needs and aspiration of all countries, and especially the adverse effect on the attainment of economic and social development objectives which may be caused by restrictive business practices arising out of transfer of technology, parties to a technology transfer transaction should refrain from the following restrictive business practices relating to the use of patents and/or know-how licences as well as to the use of trade mark licences including patents and/or know-how:

(i) Restrictions preventing the exploitation of patented technology after the expiration or invalidation of the patent or patents covering such technology, or requiring royalties to be paid for the use of patents after expiration or invalidation, provided that this shall not affect obligations undertaken in respect to know-how or the fulfilment of obligations relating to use when the patent was in force;

(ii) Prohibitions or restrictions on the use of the technology after the expiration of the arrangement, unless the technology is still legally protected, or has not legitimately entered the public domain;

(iii) Unreasonably preventing the licensee from entering into sales or representation agreements related to similar or competing technology or products or from obtaining competing technology, unless such provisions are justified, for instance, in order to secure the confidentiality of the licensed information, to give effect to best efforts or promotional obligations, or to maintain the specially close and continuous relationship between the licensor and licensee, and should refrain from the following restrictive business practices relating to the use of patent or know-how licences;

(iv) Unreasonably requiring the licensee to refrain from challenging the validity of a patent involved in the transfer or the validity of other patents owned by the licensor, recognizing that the licensor may retain the right to terminate the agreement upon the initiation of a challenge to the licensed patent's validity;

(v) Unreasonably requiring the acquiring party to grant exclusive sales or representation rights to the supplying party, unless justified, for instance, because the licence is solely for manufacturing purposes or unreasonably requiring exclusive sales or representation rights with respect to products or technology not covered by the licence;

(vi) Requiring the licensee to transfer or grant-back to the licensor exclusive rights in improvements discovered in the working of the subject matter of the licence, without offsetting consideration or reciprocal obligation, or when this practice will abuse a dominant position of the licensor;

(vii) Unreasonably restricting research or development by the licensee;

(viii) Unreasonably restricting adaptation or innovation of the technology by the licensee, unless such provisions are justified, for instance, to give effect to guarantees, to maintain the reputation of the licensor or to maintain quality of products supplied to the licensor, his affiliates, customers or other licensees;

(ix) Unreasonably requiring the licensee to use personnel designated by the licensor unless such provisions are justified, for instance, to ensure the efficient transfer of technology and its putting into practice;

(x) Restrictions unreasonably regulating prices charged by competing licensees in their home countries or in other countries where the products or their method of manufacture are not legally protected;

(xi) Provisions having the effect of unreasonably tying to transferred technology the purchase of a product or other technology, that is which oblige or impel the licensee to accept unwanted licences, or to purchase unwanted goods or services from the licensor or his designated source; unless such provisions are justified, for instance, to meet the requirements of a guarantee or to maintain quality to protect the licensor's reputation;

(xii) Restrictions which unreasonably limit the export of products or components not the subject of the transferred know-how or related industrial property right, or restrictions of unreasonable duration or scope relating to export to countries where the product or its method of manufacture is not legally protected;

(xiii) Restrictions in patent pool or cross-licensing agreements which unreasonably impose territorial, quantity or price restrictions or attempt to dominate an industry, market or new industrial process.

Chapter VI. International Collaboration and Special Measures for Developing Countries

International collaboration

6.1. International collaboration among all Governments and international organizations should be increased to encourage and facilitate an expanded international flow of technology. Such collaboration on a multilateral or bilateral basis, should take, *inter alia*, the following forms:

(i) Exchange of information leading to development and improvement of national legislation dealing with technology transfer. The present guidelines and principles could serve as a guide to the formulation of such legislation and help to establish harmonization, where appropriate, of national laws and policies in the area of technology transfer;

(ii) Facilitation of the development of scientific and technological resources of recipient enterprises including, wherever practicable, the training of recipient enterprise employees and the establishment of facilities in recipient countries which will stimulate the development of indigenous technologies;

(iii) Exchange of available information and experience in seeking solutions to problems arising out of restrictive business practices in the transfer of technology;

(iv) Provision, to the extent practicable, to recipient countries of appropriate information regarding the availability, description, and location of technologies;

(v) Co-operation to develop appropriate systems for the legal protection of industrial rights and co-operation in exchanging information and experience in the transfer of these rights and the administration of these systems. To this same end, entrance into and accession to appropriate international agreements, and review of the operation of such agreements to take account of changed circumstances. Such agreements should provide equitable treatment for both source and recipient enterprises and governments;

(vi) Action through international arrangements to avoid, as far as possible, imposition of double taxation on earnings and payments arising out of technology transfer arrangements.

Special measures for developing countries

6.2. Governments of developed countries directly or through appropriate international organizations, in order to facilitate and encourage the growth of scientific and technological capabilities of developing countries so as to assist them in their efforts to fulfil their economic and social objectives, should take the following special measures for developing countries:

(i) Facilitate access by developing countries to information regarding the availability, description and location of technologies which might help those countries to attain their economic and social development objectives;

(ii) Facilitate the access to technology covered by industrial property rights held by governments of developed countries;

(iii) Assist developing countries in the development of indigenous technologies by facilitating access to publicly available scientific and industrial research data;

(iv) Encourage the development of scientific and technological resources in developing countries, including the creation of innovative capacities;

(v) Encourage the adaptation of R & D activities to conditions and factor endowments prevailing in developing countries;

(vi) Encourage the training of personnel from developing countries.

6.3. Governments of developed countries directly or through appropriate international organizations in assisting in the transfer of technology to the developing countries should within their official development assistance programmes take into account the request from developing countries to:

(i) Contribute to the development of indigenous technologies in developing countries by providing experts under development assistance and industrial research exchange programmes;

(ii) Train scientific and industrial research personnel engaged in the development of indigenous technologies in developing countries;

(iii) Provide training in the development and administration of laws and regulations relating to the international transfer of technology and to the provision of general assistance and advice in this field;

(iv) Provide support to national institutions in developing and developed countries and to projects for the development of new and the adaptation of existing technologies suitable to the particular needs of developing countries;

(v) Provide assistance for the co-operation between scientific and technological institutions in the developed and developing countries for common R & D projects;

(vi) Extend or strengthen assistance for the establishment of national, regional and/or international institutions, including technology transfer centres, to help the developing countries to obtain the technology required for the establishment, construction and operation of plants.

6.4. The special measures to developing countries should be accorded with particular consideration for the special problems and conditions of the least developed among the developing countries.

Chapter VII. Applicable Law and Settlement of Disputes

7.1. The parties to a technology transfer agreement should be permitted freely to choose the law governing the validity, performance and interpretation of the agreement, provided that the State whose law is chosen either has a substantial relationship to the parties or to the transaction or there is other reasonable basis for the parties' choice. The parties should also be permitted to leave the issue of governing law for decision by the forum before which a dispute relating to a transfer of technology is tried.

7.2. In the absence of an effective choice of law by the parties, the substantive law governing the validity, performance and interpretation of the agreement should be that of the State which has the most significant relationship to the transaction and the parties, taking into account the following contacts:

(i) Place of performance;

(ii) Location of subject matter of contract;

(iii) Place of contracting;

(iv) Domicile, residence, nationality, place of incorporation and place of business parties;

(v) Place of negotiation.

7.3. The parties to a technology transfer agreement should be freely permitted to choose the forum before which disputes relating to the agreement shall be tried, and any such choice should be given effect unless there is no reasonable basis for the selection and the choice places an onerous burden on one of the parties.

7.4. Parties to a technology transfer agreement should be permitted to provide in such agreements for the settlement, by arbitration or other third-party procedures, of disputes related to the agreement and any such choice should be given effect except where it was in violation of the law governing the agreement at the time such agreement was entered into.

7.5. Governments should endeavour to take all possible steps to promote the equitable resolution of disputes relating to technology transfer agreements, including:

(i) Adherence to and use, where appropriate, of the facilities of the International Centre for the Settlement of Investment Disputes;

(ii) The establishment or strengthening of mechanisms in their respective judicial systems for enforcing decisions resulting from third-party dispute settlement arrangements and, to this same end, adherence to the United Nations Convention on the Recognition and Enforcement of Foreign Arbitral Awards.

Chapter VIII. Nature of the Guidelines

8.1. These guidelines are set forth in order that Governments may make known those standards which they believe should form the basis of the relationships between enterprises, between enterprises and source and recipient governments and between such governments themselves in the area of transfer of technology.

8.2. These guidelines are voluntary and legally non-binding. The guidelines neither alter nor in any way supersede national or international law nor the responsibilities of States thereunder or as set forth in international treaties or agreements.

8.3. The failure of parties to a mutually agreed technology transfer agreement to observe one or more of the guidelines should not, in and of itself, invalidate such agreement.

Appendix C

Annotated Outline for a UN Code of Conduct

The Intergovernmental Working Group on a Code of Conduct requested its Chairman to present suggestions for an annotated outline.

The Chairman's suggestions are based on the following considerations as regards the nature of the annotated outline.

- The language used should to the extent possible be neutral and descriptive and not include formulations of a legal, normative or imperative character.

- The annotations should be brief, specific and related to the items relevant to the formulation of a code. They should have the form of subheadings and key concepts rather than detailed, analytic comments. They should not be considered as conclusive.

- The annotated outline should concentrate on matters relevant to the activities of transnational corporations.

- The annotated outline should reflect the concerns of both host and home countries. Particular attention should be paid to the developing countries.

- The main headings as well as individual principles and issues included in the annotated outline should be considered in the broader context of a code. The interrelationship between different principles and issues should be recognized. Cross references between different parts of the annotated outline should be indicated in general terms. These cross references apply to specific annotations where appropriate.

- Work relevant to the tasks of the Intergovernmental Working Group is being pursued in other international bodies. Such work may yield results that should be taken into account in the formulation of the code. The results achieved by other international bodies should not, however, preclude the Working Group from reaching its own conclusions.

- Although agreement exists on annotations to a number of principles and issues it is recognized that consensus cannot be reached on all points at this stage. Consequently, the Chairman's suggestions for an outline include annotations which are not mutually consistent. The resulting incompatibilities in the text will have to be eliminated at a later stage.

- The outline should not include annotations as regards the legal nature and scope of the code or its implementation as the Working Group has decided not to deal with these matters until the substantive issues have been further explored.

- Neither the outline, nor the annotations should prejudice the positions of delegations with regard to the principles and issues to be included and the language to be used in the final formulation of the code.

I. Preamble and objectives

- It is recognized that a conclusive discussion on the annotation to the preamble and objectives cannot take place until the other issues, to be dealt with in the code have been explored in greater detail. The following annotations are preliminary, and no attempts have been made to arrange them in order.

- Declaration and Programme of Action for the Establishment of a New International Economic Order: General Assembly resolutions 3201 (S-VI) and 3202 (S-VI) of 1 May 1974; in particular relevant provisions on transnational corporations.

- Relevant parts of the Charter of Economic Rights and Duties of States: General Assembly resolution 3281 (XXIX) of 12 December 1974.

- Relevant parts of the Lima Declaration and Plan of Action on Industrial Development and Co-operation adopted by the Second General Conference of UNIDO, 26 March 1975.

- Paragraph 6 (b) of the report of the Commission on Transnational Corporations on its second session.*

- General Assembly resolution 1803 (XVII) on permanent sovereignty over natural resources.

- Particular attention to developing countries as regards the activities of transnational corporations.

II. Definitions

- The need to define transnational corporations as well as some other fundamental concepts for the purposes of a code is recognized.

- An approach similar to that in the Report of the Eminent Persons, while leaving open the possibility of developing narrower and more

---

* To secure effective international arrangements for the operation of transnational corporations designed to promote their contribution to national development goals and world economic growth while controlling and eliminating their negative effects.

specific definitions as required in the course of the formulation of a code and taking into account the further work of the Commission on these issues. These further considerations by the Working Group and the Commission might identify certain criteria regarding the definition of transnational corporations.

- The usefulness to take into account the work on definitions in other international bodies dealing with matters related to transnational corporations is recognized.

III. Major principles and/or issues related to the activities of transnational corporations

A. *General and political*

1. *Respect for national sovereignty and observance of domestic laws, regulations and administrative practices*

   - Respect by transnational corporations for national sovereignty, and the right of each State to exercise full permanent sovereignty over its wealth, resources and economic activities.

   - Observance by transnational corporations of laws, regulations and administrative practices in the countries in which they operate.

   - Respect by transnational corporations of the right of Governments to regulate and exert jurisdiction over the activities of corporations operating within their jurisdiction.

2. *Adherence to economic goals and development objectives, policies and priorities*

   - Respect by transnational corporations for and contribution to economic goals and development objectives, policies and priorities of the countries in which they operate, with particular attention to the developing countries.

   - Association by transnational corporations with and positive contribution to the development of efforts of host countries both in the national and the regional integration contexts.

   - Consistency of transnational corporation strategies and operations with explicit priorities of host countries and consultations with government authorities regarding appropriate ways to maximize contributions to the development process *inter alia* by establishing mutually beneficial relationships and compatibility of interest of transnational corporations with those of host countries.

   - Responsiveness of transnational corporations to government measures to deal with short-term national problems.

   - Renegotiability of contracts to which transnational corporations are parties, in connexion with national development plans and regional integration arrangements.

3. *Adherence to socio-cultural objectives and values*

   - Compatibility of activities of transnational corporations with the socio-cultural objectives and values of host countries and co-operation by transnational corporations with Governments of host countries with a view to ensuring that no alien elements which might adversely affect the cultural identity of host countries be transplanted.

4. *Respect for human rights and fundamental freedoms*

- Respect by transnational corporations for human rights and fundamental freedoms.

- Non-collaboration by transnational corporations with racist minority régimes in southern Africa.

5. *Non-interference in internal political affairs*

- Non-interference by transnational corporations in the internal political affairs of countries in which they operate by resorting to subversive activities, attempting to overthrow Governments or altering the political and social systems.

- Abstention by transnational corporations from activities of a political nature considered unacceptable by the laws of the country concerned and from other non-permissible activities of that kind, defined by the countries, in which they operate.

- Abstention by transnational corporations from acting as vehicles for the political interests of home, host or other countries, unless their operations in that respect are in line with the interest of all the countries concerned.

6. *Non-interference in intergovernmental relations*

- Non-interference by transnational corporations in affairs which are properly the concern of Governments.

- Abstention by transnational corporations from requesting their home Governments to exert pressure on host Governments beyond normal diplomatic representation.

- Exhaustion by transnational corporations of means available in host countries for resolving disputes before seeking diplomatic support by their home Governments in accordance with international practice.

7. *Abstention from corrupt practices*

- Abstention by transnational corporations from corrupt practices, which may include bribery, illicit payments and other corrupt practices, in countries in which they operate.

- Account to be taken of General Assembly resolution 3514 and ECOSOC resolution 2041 as well as the current work of the *Ad Hoc* Intergovernmental Working Group on the Problem of Corrupt Practices.

Cross reference to III-B, C and IV

B. *Economic, financial and social*

1. *Ownership and control*

- It is recognized that both legal aspects of ownership and the actual division of decision-making power among the different entities of a transnational corporation will have to be considered when formulating the code.

- Effective participation of nationals in the decision-making process of affiliates and subsidiaries of transnational corporations established in their territories.

- Participation of local capital in joint ventures where appropriate.

2. *Balance of payments*

- Co-operation of transnational corporations with Governments regarding the achievement of established balance-of-payments objectives with particular attention to balance-of-payments policies of the least developed countries as well as developing countries, whose economies depend on one or a few commodities.

- Contribution by transnational corporations to the balance of payments in the countries in which they operate, taking into account *inter alia* factors related to exports and imports as well as use of local and foreign financing.

- Repatriation by transnational corporations of capital and remittance of profits, royalties and fees.

- Reinvestment by transnational corporations of profits made in the countries in which they operate.

- Excessive or untimely outflows of earnings as well as intragroup capital transactions by transnational corporations, which may aggravate balance-of-payment problems in the countries in which they operate.

- Speculative capital movements by transnational corporations, that may aggravate balance-of-payments problems or currency stability in the countries in which they operate.

3. *Transfer pricing*

- Use by transnational corporations of intragroup pricing policies which reflect international market prices or are based on the "arms length" or other appropriate principles.

- Effects of transfer pricing on revenues, balance of payments and competition in the countries in which transnational corporations operate.

- Provision by transnational corporations upon request and in confidence, of relevant information on transfer prices and intragroup pricing policies to government authorities.

4. *Taxation*

- Provision by transnational corporations of relevant information for tax purposes to government authorities subject to suitable safeguards with regard to confidentiality.

- Account to be taken of work conducted by the United Nations Group on Tax Treaties and the role of bilateral and, as appropriate, multilateral, tax treaties.

5. *Competition and restrictive business practices*

   - Efforts by transnational corporations to promote competition in national and international markets.

   - Restrictive business practices by transnational corporations which adversely affect competition and which are not accepted under national or international provisions.

   - Anti-competitive behaviour by transnational corporations by abusing dominant market positions.

   - Account to be taken of the work in UNCTAD and other international bodies on restrictive business practices.

6. *Transfer of technology*

   - Contribution by transnational corporations to the scientific and technological development of the countries in which they operate.

   - Appropriate participation by transnational corporations in the transfer of technology to developing countries.

   - Account to be taken of the work on a code of conduct on transfer of technology in UNCTAD.

7. *Employment and labour*

   - Relevance of ILO principles and standards regarding *inter alia* employment promotion and security, discrimination of employees, training of local employees, replacement of foreign citizens by national citizens in management at all levels, wages, working conditions, safety and health, freedom of association, trade union rights and collective bargaining and measures in case of lay-offs, closures of plants and shifts in production.

   - Account to be taken of relevant work in ILO on matters pertaining to employment and labour, in particular of the work on a Tripartite Declaration of Principles Concerning Multinational Enterprises and Social Policy.

8. *Consumer protection*

   - Co-operation of transnational corporations with Governments with regard to the protection of consumers' health and safety and respect by transnational corporations for national and, as appropriate, international standards of quality, pricing and promotion of products.

   - Provision by transnational corporations of information to host Governments on experimental use of products and of prohibitions, restrictions and warnings imposed elsewhere on grounds of health and safety of products which they market or propose to market in host countries.

   - Provision by transnational corporations of appropriate information to the public on the contents and possible hazardous effects of products by supplying accurate labelling and by avoiding misleading advertising.

   - Co-operation of transnational corporations with Governments with a view to promote the development and sales of products which meet basic needs of the consumers.

9. *Environmental protection*

- Co-operation of transnational corporations with Governments regarding the protection, preservation and improvement of the environment and respect by transnational corporations for national and international standards in this field.

- Provisions by transnational corporations of information about the environmental effects of production processes they use or intend to use and on restrictions imposed on similar activities elsewhere on grounds of environmental protection.

- Account of work in UNEP and other international bodies on the development of international environmental protection standards.

Cross reference to III A and C and IV

C. *Disclosure of information*

- Provision by transnational corporations of information to the public on their activities as a whole, broken down by geographical area or country and major lines of business as appropriate, to complement information required under national law and in the countries in which they operate. Taking account of requirements of business confidentiality, the effect on the competitive position of transnational corporations concerned and the cost of producing the information, such information might include *inter alia*: structure of the transnational corporation, financial statements, sources and uses of funds, employment, investment, etc. together with statements on transfer pricing policies and the accounting principles used in compiling and consolidating the information. In providing a suitable breakdown of information, account to be taken of the significance of the transnational corporation operations in a particular country or group of countries and the links with operations in other countries.

- Supply by transnational corporations of information to affiliates and subsidiaries in order to enable them to meet the needs of Governments for information, including that which may be held in other countries, required for legislative and administrative purposes, regarding *inter alia* taxation, exports and imports, transfer pricing, contribution to development objectives, restrictive business practices and monitoring as well as for incorporation in statistics, taking account of requirements for commercial confidentiality.

- Provision by transnational corporations to representatives of employees of information needed for meaningful negotiations taking into account national, and where appropriate, international standards and practices.

- Account of the work of the Expert Group on the Development of International Standards of Accounting and Reporting and of the activities of the Centre on Transnational Corporations as regards information as well as of work pursued by other international bodies in this field.

IV. Principles and/or issues relating to the treatment of transnational corporations

- Intergovernmental co-operation in matters related to the activities of transnational corporations, in preventing and combating corrupt practices, in exchanging information regarding transfer pricing, taxation and restrictive business practices, in consumer and environmental protection, in disclosure of information on transnational corporations, in jurisdictional issues and the settlement of disputes.

A. *General treatment of transnational corporations by home and host countries*

- Equitable, non-discriminatory and non-preferential treatment of affiliates and subsidiaries of transnational corporations established under the laws, regulations and administrative practices of host countries, with due regard to contractual obligations to which parties have freely subscribed and to international law and taking into account such features of transnational corporations which separate them from national enterprises and *inter alia* requirements of national security.

- Clarity and predictability of terms of admission and operation of transnational corporations, of objectives, priorities, laws, regulations and administrative practices affecting the activities of transnational corporations as well as transparency of rules and policies regarding non-permissible activities of a political nature by transnational corporations.

- Rights of transnational corporations in the application and modifications of laws, regulations and administrative practices as well as the right of transnational corporations to adequate legal protection of industrial property.

- Abstention from using transnational corporations as instruments for the attainment of government policy objectives, unless such activities correspond to the interests of all countries concerned, and from exerting pressure on other Governments on behalf of transnational corporations beyond normal diplomatic representation.

B. *Nationalization and compensation*

- Right of nationalization.
- Provision of compensation.
- Settlement of disputes and jurisdictional issues.

C. *Jurisdiction*

- Extent of jurisdiction over transnational corporation activities by Governments of the countries, in which they operate.
- Ability of parties to a contract to select governing law and forum to be used in the resolution of disputes.

- Use of impartial arbitration to resolve disputes relating to the activities of transnational corporations.
- Intergovernmental co-operation to resolve difficulties which may arise when transnational corporations are subject to conflicting requirements of Governments and in cases of extraterritorial application of law.

Cross reference to III A, B and C.

Considering that certain activities of transnational corporations may go beyond the jurisdictions of home as well as host countries and that one of the basic aims of international co-operation regarding transnational corporations is to cover such activities by international arrangements which supplement national law and jurisdiction, a cross reference is made to VI.

V. Legal nature and scope

(See introductory notes.)

VI. Implementation

(See introductory notes.)

Bibliography

Aitken, Bruce. "Multinational Enterprises and International Law: A Selected Bibliography." *International Lawyer* (1977) 11: 69–100.

Armstrong, Frances. "Political Components and Practical Effects of the Andean Foreign Investment Code." *Stanford Law Review* (July 1975) 27: 1597–1628.

Avery, William P. "Oil, Politics and Economic Policy Making: Venezuela and the Andean Common Market." *International Organization* (Autumn 1976) 30: 541–571.

Ball, George W. "The Relations of the Multinational Corporation to the 'Host' State." In George W. Ball, ed. *Global Companies.* Englewood Cliffs, N.J.: Prentice-Hall, Inc., 1975.

Bar-Lev, Joshua. "UNCTAD Code of Practice for the Regulation of Liner Conferences." *Journal of Maritime Law and Commerce* (July 1972) 3: 783–791.

Bosies, William J., Jr., and Green, William G. "The Liner Conference Convention: Launching an International Regulatory Regime." *Law and Policy in International Business* (1974) 6: 533–574.

Brower, Charles N., and Tepe, John B., Jr. "The Charter of Economic Rights and Duties of States: A Reflection or Rejection of International Law." *International Lawyer* (1975) 9: 295–318.

Capone, Ronald A. "U.S. Laws and the Convention on a Code of Conduct for Liner Conferences: A Catalogue of Conflicts and Dilemmas." *Virginia Journal of International Law* (Winter 1975) 15: 249–276.

"Chilean Tremors Shake the Andean Pact." *Multinational Business* (1976) 4: 8–14.

Coonrod, Stephen. "The United Nations Code of Conduct for Transnational Corporations." *Harvard International Law Journal* (Spring 1977) 18: 273–307.

Davidow, Joel. "U.S. Antitrust Laws and International Transfers of Technology—The Government View." *Fordham Law Review* (April 1975) 43: 733–740.

Ebb, Lawrence F. "Transfers of Foreign Technology in Latin America: The Birth of Antitrust Law?" *Fordham Law Review* (April 1975) 43: 719–732.

Falk, Richard A. "On the Quasi-Legislative Competence of the General Assembly." *American Journal of International Law* (1966) 60: 782–791.

Farthing, R.B.C. "UNCTAD Code of Practice for the Regulation of Liner Conferences—Another View." *Journal of Maritime Law and Commerce* (April 1973) 4: 467–473.

Fatouros, A.A. "An International Care to Protect Private Investment—Proposals and Perspectives." *University of Toronto Law Journal* (1961) 14: 77–102.

Fatouros, A.A. "The Computer and the Mud Hut: Notes on Multinational Enterprise in Developing Countries." *Columbia Journal of Transnational Law* (1971) 10: 325–363.

Feld, Werner J. "U.N. Supervision Over MNCs: Realistic Expectation or Exercise in Futility?" *Orbis* (Winter 1976) 19: 1499–1518.

Fisher, Bart S. "The Multinationals and the Crisis in United States Trade and Investment Policy." *Boston University Law Review* (1973) 53: 308–366.

Fouts, S.F. "Andean Foreign Investment Code." *Texas International Law Journal* (1975) 10: 537–559.

Furnish, Dale B. "A Transnational Approach to Restrictive Business Practices." *International Lawyer* (1970) 4: 317–351.

Goldberg, Paul M., and Kindleberger, Charles P. "Toward a GATT for Investment: A Proposal for Supervision of the International Corporation." *Law and Policy in International Business* (1970) 2: 295–325.

Heldt, Sven. "The Decay of the Andean Group." *Intereconomics* (1977) 3/4: 72–78.

"How Will Multinational Firms React to the Andean Pact's Decision 24?" *Inter-American Economic Affairs* (Autumn 1971) 25: 55–65.

Jansson, Jan Owen. "Intra-Tariff Cross-Subsidization in Liner Shipping." *Journal of Transport Economics and Policy* (September 1974): 294–311.

Jeffries, Countess Pease. "Regulation of Transfer of Technology: An Evaluation of the UNCTAD Code of Conduct." *Harvard International Law Journal* (Spring 1977) 18: 309–342.

Joelson, Mark R. "The Proposed International Codes of Conduct as Related to Restrictive Business Practices." *Law and Policy in International Business* (1976) 8: 837–874.

Joelson, Mark R., and Griffin, Joseph P. "International Regulation of Restrictive Business Practices Engaged in by Transnational Enterprises: A Prognosis." *International Lawyer* (1977) 11: 5–28.

Keohane, Robert O., and Ooms, Van Doorn. "The Multinational Firm and International Regulation." *International Organization* (Winter 1975) 29: 169–209.

Kindleberger, Charles P. "The Multinational Corporation in a World of Militant Developing Countries." In George W. Ball, ed. *Global Companies.* Englewood Cliffs, N.J.: Prentice-Hall Inc., 1975.

Lisocki, Stanley R. "The Andean Investment Code." *Notre Dame Lawyer* (December 1973) 49: 317–333.

Metzger, Stanley D. "Cartels, Combines, Commodity Agreements and International Law." *Texas International Law Journal* (1976) 11: 527–539.

Mirabito, A. J. "Control of Technology Transfer: The Burke-Hartke Legislation and the Andean Foreign Investment Code." *International Lawyer* (April 1975) 9: 215–238.

Muller, Ronald. "A Qualifying and Dissenting View of the Multinational Corporation." In George W. Ball, ed. *Global Companies*. Englewood Cliffs, N.J.: Prentice-Hall Inc., 1975.

Nader, Ralph; Green, Mark, and Seligman, Joel. *Taming the Giant Corporation*. New York: W. W. Norton & Co., Inc., 1976.

Nye, J.S., and Rubin, Seymour J. "The Longer Range Political Role of the Multinational Corporation." In George W. Ball, ed. *Global Companies*. Englewood Cliffs, N.J.: Prentice-Hall Inc., 1975.

Oliver, Covey T. "The Andean Foreign Investment Code: A New Phase in the Quest for Normative Order as to Direct Foreign Investment." *American Journal of International Law* (1972) 66: 763–784.

Perlmutter, Howard V. "Perplexing Routes to M.N.E. Legitimacy: Codes of Conduct for Technology Transfer." *Stanford Journal of International Studies* (Spring 1976) 11: 169–199.

Pisar, Samuel. "Trade Law and Peace: A Model Code for East-West Transactions." *International Law and Economics* (August-December 1975) 10: 267–289.

Rogers, William D. "United States Investment in Latin America: A Critical Appraisal." *Virginia Journal of International Law* (1971) 11: 246–255.

Rose, Stanley F. "The Andean Pact and Its Foreign Investment Code—Need for Clarity?" *Tax Management-International Journal* (January 1975) 1: 3–16.

Rosenstein-Rodan, P.N. "Problems of Industrialization of Eastern and South-Eastern Europe." *The Economic Journal* (June-September 1943) 53: 203–211.

Ross-Skinner, Jean. "The Growing Power of OECD." *Dun's Review* (September 1976) 108: 93–94.

Rostow, Eugene V. "The Multinational Corporation and the Future of the World Economy." In George W. Ball, ed. *Global Companies*. Englewood Cliffs, N.J.: Prentice-Hall Inc., 1975.

Rostow, Eugene; Nye, Joseph, and Ball, George. "The Need for International Arrangements." In George W. Ball, ed. *Global Companies*. Englewood Cliffs, N.J.: Prentice-Hall Inc., 1975.

Rubin, Seymour J. "Developments in the Law and Institutions of International Economic Relations." *American Journal of International Law* (1976) 70: 73–91.

Rubin, Seymour J. "Harmonization of Rules: A Perspective on the U. N. Commission on Transnational Corporations." *Law and Policy in International Business* (1976) 8: 875–893.

Rubin, Seymour J. "The Multinational Enterprise and the 'Home' State." In George W. Ball, ed. *Global Companies*. Englewood Cliffs, N.J.: Prentice-Hall Inc., 1975.

Rubin, Seymour J. "Report on the Düsseldorf Conference on International Controls on Foreign Investment." *International Lawyer* (1973) 7: 825–829.

Salzman, Herbert. "How to Reduce and Manage the Political Risks of Investment in Less Developed Countries." In George W. Ball, ed. *Global Companies*. Englewood Cliffs, N.J.: Prentice-Hall Inc., 1975.

Schachter, Oscar. "Twilight Existence of Nonbinding International Agreements." *American Journal of International Law* (April 1977) 71: 296–304.

Schill, Charles F. "The Mexican and Andean Investment Codes: An Overview and Comparison." *Law and Policy in International Business* (1974) 6: 437–483.

Schuessler, Robert, and Spiller, David. "Report on the Economic Impacts of the UNCTAD Code of Conduct for Liner Conferences." U.S. Department of Transportation, 1975.

Shah, M. J. "The Dispute Settlement Machinery in the Convention on a Code of Conduct for Liner Conferences." *Journal of Maritime Law and Commerce* (October 1975) 7: 127–168.

Solomon, Lewis D. "Multinational Corporations and the Emerging World Order." *Case Western Reserve Journal of International Law* (Spring 1976) 8: 329–428.

Tharp, Paul A., Jr. "Transnational Enterprises and International Regulation: A Survey of Various Approaches in International Organizations." *International Organization* (Winter 1976) 30: 47–73.

Thomas, Larry W. "The Colombian Supreme Court Decision on the Andean Foreign Investment Code and Its Implications for the Law of Treaties." *Journal of International Law and Economics* (June 1973) 8: 113–128.

Tresselt, Dag. "The Controversy over the Division of Labour in International Seaborne Transport." Bergen: Institute for Shipping Research, 1970.

United Nations, Centre on Transnational Corporations. *The CTC Reporter*. December 1976.

United Nations, Centre on Transnational Corporations. *The CTC Reporter*. June 1977.

United Nations, Centre on Transnational Corporations. *Transnational Corporations: Issues Involved in the Formulation of a Code of Conduct* (E/C. 10/17). 1976.

United Nations, Centre on Transnational Corporations. *Transnational Corporations: Material Relevant to the Formulation of a Code of Conduct* (E/C.10/18). 1977.

United Nations, Conference on Trade and Development. *The Impact of Trade Marks on the Development Process of Developing Countries* (TD/B/C.6/AC.3/3). June 29, 1977.

United Nations, Conference on Trade and Development. *Preparation of a*

Draft Outline of an International Code of Conduct on Transfer of Technology (TD/B/C.6/AC.1/2). March 25, 1975.

United Nations, Conference on Trade and Development. *Report of the Ad Hoc Group of Experts on Restrictive Business Practices in Relation to the Trade and Development of Developing Countries* (TD/B/C.2/119/Rev. 1). 1974.

United Nations, Conference on Trade and Development. *Report of the Intergovernmental Group of Experts on an International Code of Conduct on Transfer of Technology on Its Third Session* (TD/AC.1/9). 1977.

United Nations, Conference on Trade and Development. *United Nations Conference of Plenipotentiaries on a Code of Conduct for Liner Conferences: Final Act and Annexes* (TD/CODE/11/Rev.1). May 9, 1974.

United Nations, Conference on Trade and Development. *United Nations Conference of Plenipotentiaries on a Code of Conduct for Liner Conferences: Statements by Delegations* (SHC/CODE/85). April 22, 1974.

United Nations, Economic and Social Council. *Commission on Transnational Corporations Report of the Resumed Second Session and the Third Session (3 March and 25 April–6 May 1977). Supplement No. 5* (E/C.10/32).

United Nations, Economic and Social Council. *The Impact of Multinational Corporations on Development and on International Relations* (E/5500/ Rev. 1/ST/ESA/6). 1974.

United Nations, Economic and Social Council. *International Codes and Regional Agreements Relating to Transnational Corporations* (E/C.10/9). January 30, 1976.

United Nations, Economic and Social Council. *International Codes and Regional Agreements Relating to Transnational Corporations* (E/C. 10/9/Add. 1). February 3, 1976.

United Nations, Economic and Social Council. *Official Records. Resumed 57th Session: 14 and 18 October, 19, 26, 29 November and 5, 10, and 16 December 1974. Resolutions. Supplement No. 1A* (E/5570/Add. 1).

United Nations, Economic and Social Council. *Proposed Programme of Technical Co-Operation on Matters Related to Transnational Corporations* (E/C.10/13). January 28, 1976.

United Nations, Economic and Social Council. *Transnational Corporations: Views and Proposals of Non-Governmental Interests on a Code of Conduct* (E/C.10/20). December 30, 1976.

United Nations, Economic and Social Council. *Transnational Corporations: Views and Proposals of States on a Code of Conduct* (E/C.10/19). December 30, 1976.

United Nations, Economic and Social Council. *Transnational Corporations: Views and Proposals of States on a Code of Conduct* (E/C.10/19 Add. 1). March 22, 1977.

United Nations, General Assembly. *Work Related to the Formulation of a Code of Conduct: Report of the Intergovernmental Working Group on a Code of Conduct* (E/C.10/31), May 4, 1977.

USA-BIAC Committee on International Investment and Multinational Enterprise. *A Discussion of Provision of Data on MNC Operations*. November 1974.

USA-BIAC Committee on International Investment and Multinational Enterprise. *A Review of the Declaration on International Investment and Multinational Enterprises*. November 1976.

U.S. Congress, House of Representatives, Committee on Interstate and Foreign Commerce, *H.R. 12040. A Bill to amend the Securities Exchange Act of 1934 to prevent control by foreign persons of American companies engaged in vital industries*, 93rd Congress, 1st session, December 19, 1973.

U.S. Congress, Senate, Committee on Banking, Housing and Urban Affairs, *S. 953. A Bill to amend the Export Administration Act of 1969 to clarify and strengthen the authority of the Secretary of Commerce to take action in the case of restrictive trade practices or boycotts*, 94th Congress, 2nd session, February 6, 1976.

U.S. Congress, Senate, Committee on Banking, Housing and Urban Affairs, *S. 3084. A Bill to extend the Export Administration Act of 1969, as amended*, 94th Congress, 2nd session, March 4, 1976.

Vagts, Detlev F. "The Host Country Faces the Multinational Enterprise." *Boston University Law Review* (1973) 53: 261–277.

Vagts, Detlev F. "The Multinational Enterprise: A New Challenge for Transnational Law." *Harvard Law Review* (1970) 83: 739–792.

Valdez, Abelardo Lopez. "The Andean Foreign Investment Code: An Analysis." *Journal of International Law and Economics* (June 1972) 7: 1–19.

Von Mehren, Robert B., and Gold, Martin E. "Multinational Corporations: Conflicts and Controls." *Stanford Journal of International Studies* (Spring 1976) 11: 1–41.

Wang, Nian Tzu. "The Design of an International Code of Conduct for Transnational Corporations." *Journal of International Law and Economics* (1975) 10: 319–336.

Wilner, Gabriel M. "Survey of the Activities of UNCTAD and UNCITRAL in the Field of International Legislation on Shipping." *Journal of Maritime Law and Commerce* (October 1971) 3: 129–144.

Zamora, Antonio R. "Andean Common Market—Regulation of Foreign Investments: Blueprint for the Future?" *International Lawyer* 10: 153–166.

Zamora, Stephen. "Rate Regulation in Ocean Transport: Developing Countries Confront the Liner Conference System." *California Law Review* (1971) 59: 1299–1332.

Zaphiriou, G. A. "International Code of Conduct on Transfer of Technology." *International and Comparative Law Quarterly* (January 1977) 26: 210–218.

SELECTED AEI PUBLICATIONS

The Constitution and the Budget, W.S. Moore and Rudolph G. Penner, eds. (172 pp., paper $6.25, cloth $14.25)

Foreign Intelligence: Legal and Democratic Controls, Peter Hackes, mod. (37 pp., $3.75)

Religion and Politics: The Intentions of the Authors of the First Amendment, Michael J. Malbin (40 pp., $2.25)

Women and Social Security: An Institutional Dilemma, Marilyn R. Flowers (41 pp., $2.25)

Significant Decisions of the Supreme Court, Bruce E. Fein.

1971–1972 Term (65 pp., $2)

1972–1973 Term (136 pp., $3)

1973–1974 Term (148 pp., $3)

1974–1975 Term (148 pp., $3)

1975–1976 Term (198 pp., $4.75)

1976–1977 Term (168 pp., $3.75)

1977–1978 Term (162 pp., $6.25)

1978–1979 Term (199 pp., $6.25)

Prices subject to change without notice.

AEI ASSOCIATES PROGRAM

The American Enterprise Institute invites your participation in the competition of ideas through its AEI Associates Program. This program has two objectives:

The first is to broaden the distribution of AEI studies, conferences, forums, and reviews, and thereby to extend public familiarity with the issues. AEI Associates receive regular information on AEI research and programs, and they can order publications and cassettes at a savings.

The second objective is to increase the research activity of the American Enterprise Institute and the dissemination of its published materials to policy makers, the academic community, journalists, and others who help shape public attitudes. Your contribution, which in most cases is partly tax deductible, will help ensure that decision makers have the benefit of scholarly research on the practical options to be considered before programs are formulated. The issues studied by AEI include:

- Defense Policy
- Economic Policy
- Energy Policy
- Foreign Policy
- Government Regulation
- Health Policy
- Legal Policy
- Political and Social Processes
- Social Security and Retirement Policy
- Tax Policy

For more information, write to:

AMERICAN ENTERPRISE INSTITUTE
1150 Seventeenth Street, N.W.
Washington, D.C. 20036

A Note on the Book

The typeface used for the text of this book is Palatino, designed by Hermann Zapf. The type was set by Maryland Linotype Composition Company, of Baltimore. Braun-Brumfield, Inc., of Ann Arbor, Michigan, printed and bound the book, using paper manufactured by the S. D. Warren Company. The cover and format were designed by Pat Taylor.

The manuscript was edited by David Aiken and by Lisa Skoog and Donna Spitler, of the AEI Publications Staff.